The Birds of the Falkland Islands

Robin W. Woods

The Birds of the Falkland Islands

Anthony Nelson

© 1975 Robin W. Woods
Published by Anthony Nelson, P.O. Box 9
Oswestry, Shropshire, SY11 1BY

ISBN 0 904614 00 X

Photographs by Robin W. Woods

Designed by Humphrey Stone
and printed in Great Britain at
The Compton Press Ltd., Compton Chamberlayne
Salisbury, Wiltshire

Contents

List of Tables, Figures & Maps

Foreword by Sir Peter Scott, C.B.E., D.S.C.

I greatly welcome the publication of The Birds of the Falkland Islands. It is a much needed handbook, and I am sure it will have every success.

Congratulations to the author for a clear and concise field guide, and a valuable addition to the ornithological reference library.

Peter Scott.

The New Grounds,
Slimbridge,
Gloucester GL2 7BT

Preface

Interest in the natural history of the Falkland Islands has been growing steadily in recent years amongst Falkland Islanders, other residents, and the increasing number of tourists who visit these islands each year. This book has been written for the many people who have wanted a comprehensive guide to the birds of the Falkland Islands.

The Introduction provides background information about the Islands, including notes on the physical features, climate and vegetation, with particular reference to the environment as it affects the birds. The native plant, tussock-grass, is shown to be of major importance as a habitat, and following this, there is a section which surveys the changes in vegetation since grazing began. The Introduction describes the Classification of breeding birds and comments on their distribution. The non-breeding migrants and vagrants are briefly mentioned. The effects of human activities on the bird populations are discussed, in order that the existing bird life can be seen in perspective. Finally, notes are included on recent changes in legislation which should conserve Falkland birds for the future, and should ensure that suitable habitats complete with natural vegetation are protected from exploitation.

The Key to Families and the Field Guide section are designed to help observers to identify any of the breeding birds or regular visiting species that are likely to be seen. The Field Guide also provides some information on the lives of the breeding birds as a basis for further study. The annotated list, which immediately follows the Field Guide, includes records of all birds that are known to have occurred less than five times and those species that formerly bred in the Falkland Islands. I should be grateful if readers would inform me if they consider any ornithological data to be inaccurate, and I should welcome additional records of any kind.

Acknowledgements

Travelling to distant parts of the main islands, or to the offshore islands, was not easy when I was restricted to Stanley by my work at the Meteorological Station. Therefore, I am indebted to the many people who sent bird specimens for identification, or contributed information about birds in other parts of the Islands.

I must thank Lily and Roddy Napier of West Point Island for their hospitality during two extended visits to their island. I am very grateful for all the detailed observations on Falkland birds which Roddy Napier has given me.

I thank Kitty and Cecil Bertrand of Carcass Island for the opportunity to visit their island briefly, and for some most interesting ornithological records.

I also wish to record my thanks for information or assistance received from the following people: David Bartlett: *Darwin, Stanley, Roy Cove*; Mr. and Mrs. Stan Bennett: *Stanley*; Sturdee Betts: *Keppel Island*; Mr. and Mrs. Stuart Booth: *Stanley*; Jack Bowles: *Stanley*; John Bromley: *Carcass Island, Hill Cove, Dunbar*; John Browning: *Stanley*; Tony Carey: *Stanley*; Don Davidson: *Stanley, West Point Island*; Harry Dollman: *Stanley, Kidney Island*; Norman Drake: *Port Howard*; George Edwards: *Stanley*; Jim Forbes: *Stanley, Kidney Island*; David Galloway: *Teal River, Chartres, Roy Cove, Dunbar, Carcass Island*; Dr. J. E. Hamilton: *Stanley*; Eileen and Jim Lellman: *Stanley*; Dr. and Mrs. David Marshall: *Fox Bay East*; Heather and Willy May: *West Point Island*; Mrs. Gladys Napier: *West Point Island*; Tony Nelson: *Douglas, Green Patch, Horseshoe Bay, Johnson's Harbour, Port Louis, Salvador*; Jack Newing: *Stanley*; Ron Pinder: *Kidney Island*; John Poltock: *Darwin*; Brian Powell: *Stanley, New Island*; Glyn Pugh: *Stanley*; Bob Reid: *Bleaker, George and Speedwell Islands*; Mr. and Mrs. Ted Robson: *West Point Island*; Mike Shaw: *Goose Green, Port Stephens*; Mr. and Mrs. Archie Short: *Bleaker Island*; Jim Stephenson: *Stanley*; George Stewart: *Stanley*; Ian Strange: *Stanley, Grand and Steeple Jason Islands, Beauchene Island*; Sid Summers: *Government Radio/Telephone Station Stanley*; Mark White: *Stanley*; John Winkley:

Stanley; Bruce Withers: *Stanley*; and many others too numerous to mention individually.

Acknowledgements are made to the British Antarctic Survey for permission to reproduce extracts from their synoptic meteorological charts; to John Bartholomew & Son Ltd. for permission to use part of their map on page 92 of the Readers Digest Great World Atlas; to the Controller of H.M. Stationery Office for permission to reproduce from the Directorate of Overseas Surveys' map DOS 906, and to Mrs. K. Bertrand for permission to reproduce extracts from her article 'Carcass Island 1765–1967'.

My thanks are due to Dr. Brian Roberts of the Scott Polar Research Institute, Cambridge, for a useful list of publications on birds of the Falkland Islands, and to Edwin M. Cawkell, who loaned me his typescript notes on Falkland birds. I must also thank the following British Antarctic Survey biologists who helped me in several ways; Neville Jones, Fergus O'Gorman, Mike Thurston and W. L. N. Tickell. I am particularly indebted to Lance Tickell for his critical comments and advice during the lengthy period in which I have been working on Falkland birds. Dr. O. S. Pettingill jr., who visited the Falklands in 1953/54 and again in 1971/72, has continually encouraged me, and I thank him particularly for checking the nomenclature of all species. I am very grateful to Alan Spain of Penguin Books Ltd., for early help with the illustrations. Charles J. Bridgman, M.B.O.U., has contributed enormously by his critical reading of the Field Guide section; his comments have been most valuable in eliminating ambiguities. Finally, I must thank my publisher, Tony Nelson. Without his enthusiasm the book would never have been completed.

68 Aller Park Road,   R. W. WOODS
Newton Abbot, Devon.   *August* 1974

Introduction

The Falkland Islands lie in the South Atlantic on the Patagonian Continental Shelf, between latitudes 51° and 53°S and longitudes 57°30′ and 61°30′W. They are about 350 miles from the nearest point of South America, Cape San Diego on Tierra del Fuego. The two main islands, East Falkland and West Falkland, are separated by Falkland Sound. There are about two hundred much smaller islands, the majority round the coast of West Falkland. They have a total land area of approximately 4,700 square miles.

West Falkland is generally higher and has more hills than East Falkland. It has a range of low mountains in the north running east to west. Mt. Adam, the highest peak, is 2,297 ft. above sea level. Another range, the Hornby Mountains, runs parallel to Falkland Sound. On East Falkland, north of Choiseul Sound, the land rises gently from sea level to the Wickham Heights, which reach 1,500 to 2,000 ft. generally (Mt. Usborne, 2,312 ft.) and stretch east to west across the northern half of the island. Outcrops of rock occur on most ridges and hilltops and form the higher parts of the mountains. Red-backed Hawk, Crested Caracara and Peregrine Falcon are typical birds of these crags. Lafonia, the southern part of East Falkland, is an area of remarkably low, undulating land, rarely rising above 200 ft.

Stone-runs are a unique feature of the Falkland uplands. They occur extensively on hillsides and along valleys and are formed from accumulations of large angular boulders, many being several feet across and probably weighing 50 tons or more. It is not certain how they were formed (Maling, 1960). Though stone-runs are apparently so barren, apart from lichen growth, they provide ideal nesting-sites for one species, the Dark-faced Ground-tyrant.

The coastline is deeply indented with many sheltered harbours. On the northern and eastern coasts of both main islands there are extensive beaches of near-white sand, sometimes with lagoons or ponds. Two-banded Plover and Magellanic Oystercatcher are typical of this habitat throughout the year.

ABOVE Tumbledown Mt., near Stanley.

BELOW Aerial view of stone-runs on the Wickham Heights.

13

Migrants from North America, the Sanderling and White-rumped Sandpiper, may be seen between September and April. Rocky points, headlands and boulder-strewn beaches are also regular coastal features. Typical species seen on rocky beaches are Kelp Goose, Black Oystercatcher and Night Heron. The western coast of West Falkland and its off-lying islands are rugged with some cliffs rising to 1,200 ft., meeting the full force of the South Atlantic swell and the westerly gales. Black-browed Albatross and Rockhopper Penguin nest on many of these west-facing cliffs, including those of New Island, West Point Island and Grand and Steeple Jason Islands.

The soil over most of the Falklands is peaty with underlying peat deposits up to 18 ft. thick. Clay lies beneath the peat and the ground is generally very damp and often waterlogged. There are numerous ponds (ranging in size from a few square yards to a square mile), particularly in the centre of West Falkland, in Lafonia, in northeast East Falkland and south of the Wickham Heights. Most small ponds lack plant and invertebrate life due to acidity, but in larger ponds, aquatic plants are often abundant and these ponds are favoured by several species of ducks and the two grebes. The uplands are drained by many streams and rivers, but none are navigable for any appreciable distance.

There is little cultivated land. Most houses in Stanley and the settlements have large gardens, and there are some planted gorse hedges and a few small fields of grass or oats near settlements. Peat has been the main source of fuel since settlement began, and much of Stanley Common is scarred by peat cuttings.

The land appears bleak due to the absence of native trees, but the white sand-beaches, brilliant green grass around ponds or the coastal clumps of tussock-grass, contrast pleasantly with the windswept uplands. The wide expanses of rolling straw-coloured grassland, mottled with dark patches of diddle-dee and grey rock outcrops also have an attraction of their own. The atmosphere is clear and it is often possible to see vast distances. The silence, broken only by the cries of animals and birds and the thunder of surf, the solitude, and the strong, cool winds, combine to give a sense of exhilaration and freedom. (Colour photo: p. 208)

The climate of the Falkland Islands has been much maligned in the past. It is true that often in winter it can be depressingly dull and damp, or bitterly cold with a southerly gale, but calm, frosty winter days and the many days of bright sunshine with a brisk drying wind in spring and summer, are very enjoyable.

Briefly, the climate is cool with a small temperature range, high winds, much

View over Uranie Bay, Berkeley Sound from the south.

variability from day to day and little change between seasons. These are all characteristic features of temperate oceanic climates (Maling, 1960).

Falkland weather is dominated by westerly winds, associated with the usual track of depressions through Drake Passage. Westerly gales occurring during spring and autumn often carry small birds eastwards from Tierra del Fuego or Patagonia to the Falklands. Calm periods are rare and occur more frequently in winter. The average wind speed is 15 knots (17 m.p.h.), while strong winds are frequent and gale force winds (34 knots or more) occur on about four days a month. As a result of the persistent wind, air temperatures often feel lower than they are, but this effect is alleviated by the clarity of the air and the brilliance of the sunlight. Average monthly temperatures vary between 9°C (49°F) in January and 2°C (36°F) in July. The average annual temperature is about 6°C (43°F).

Harbour road west of Stanley, under snow.

Mornings in summer often start bright and clear but shower clouds build rapidly, producing gusty winds and rain or hail by afternoon. Depressions with steady rain and strong winds also move rapidly eastwards across the Falklands. The sudden changes which occur are an annoying feature of the weather, and always have to be taken into account when travelling about the Islands by floatplane or in small boats.

The humidity of the air is generally high due to the oceanic situation and there are few completely cloudless days. The average annual precipitation is about 25 in., spread fairly evenly through the year. Snow has fallen in all months except January and February, but it rarely lies more than a few days on the lower ground.

The drying effect of the wind is most noticeable in September and October and, as there is usually less rain in these months, it is a good time for gardening

Camp track with drainage ditches near Rolon Cove.

and cutting peat. The tracks between settlements also dry out, making travel overland much easier than in winter when they are waterlogged.

It is not surprising that the cool, windy and equable climate has several marked effects on Falkland birds. Pettingill (1960) has reviewed this subject carefully, and his conclusions are summarized:

1. With the exception of seabirds, most species have a long breeding season, or start nesting very early in the spring, because there is no marked change between seasons.

2. The persistent strong winds have so limited the amount of plant cover available for land-birds, that only nine native passerine species, or 'perching birds', occur. The wind and the lack of tall vegetation have both led to a shortage of flying insects. The small number of bird species and low density of their populations is almost certainly due to the paucity of both cover and flying

insects. It is noticeable that settlements where trees and shrubs have been introduced, can support a higher density of some passerine species than the surrounding land.

3. The cool climate and consequent shortage of food cause several Falkland species to lay smaller clutches of eggs than similar species on the South American mainland.

4. The body-size of at least six of the nine Falkland races of passerines is greater than that of the equivalent South American mainland races. Larger birds have less difficulty in maintaining body heat than small birds because their surface area per unit of weight is less.

5. The lack of severe weather allows most breeding species to survive the Falkland winter. Species which could migrate are probably deterred by the westerly winds.

The Falkland seas have a great influence on the bird population. The Falkland Islands are in the Southern Cold-Temperate zone of surface water, which has here a surface temperature rarely exceeding 10°C (50°F). The cool Cape Horn Current divides southwest of the Islands and two branches of it sweep northwards as the Falkland Current to join south of Uruguay. This current penetrates northward to Rio de Janeiro (23°S), while the influence of the warm Brazil Current extends southwards to about 40°S. Marine life is abundant where these two currents mix and in the areas of upwelling water off the continental shelf north of the Falklands. The Lobster-krill is an important species that forms huge red shoals, particularly off the coasts of Patagonia, Tierra del Fuego and the Falklands. These offshore waters provide food for petrels, albatrosses and penguins. Cormorants and gulls also feed on krill when shoals are close to the shore.

The Giant Kelp beds, which are most extensive in sheltered waters between about 6 and 20 fathoms deep, round all Falkland coasts, support many crustaceans and fish which provide food for the Steamer Ducks, Rock Cormorant, three species of gull and the South American Tern.

There is no organized fishing offshore, though penguins were killed for oil, and whaling and sealing were carried out intensively at different periods in the past. The general effect of these activities on the habitat of Falkland seabirds is not known. Marine food has always been plentiful, but it is likely that scavenging species such as the gulls and Giant Petrel benefited from the large amount of offal produced.

A party of Falkland Flightless Steamer Ducks in kelp off Kidney Island.

The vegetation consists of grasses, shrubs which rarely reach 5 ft. in height, and various low plants. Natural tree growth has been prevented by the climate, the acid nature of the soil and the absence of some nitrogen-fixing bacteria. Most trees planted in or near settlements are stunted by the cold winds. There is only limited cover for birds that nest above ground level and therefore the most widespread land-birds are those adapted to ground living, such as the Black-throated Finch which feeds, sings and nests within inches of the soil.

According to Davies, who carried out the only systematic ecological survey of the Islands in 1937–8, 51% of the vegetation is of the 'Hard Camp' type and 45% is 'Soft Camp'.* The remaining 4% is made up of better quality grasslands around settlements, in valleys, on the coast particularly by large ponds, and Tussock-grass on coastal points or islands (Maling, 1960).

* Camp is derived from the spanish 'campo' meaning countryside, and is the local name for all land outside Stanley.

Crossing White grass Camp near the Lagoon.

Hard Camp is well-drained, hard ground characterized by the coarse White grass, ferns and a species of heath known as diddle-dee. Birds typical of this type of ground are the Rufous-chested Dotterel, Falkland Pipit and Long-tailed Meadowlark. (Colour photo: p. 207)

Soft Camp is covered by dense White grass, with rushes and spongy mosses in the dampest places. Typical birds are Marsh Wren and Common Snipe.

The better quality grassland is mainly of Meadow grass species. Continual grazing, trampling and manuring by livestock, ducks and geese are probably important factors in the maintenance of this type of vegetation. Magellanic and Gentoo Penguins also provide nitrogenous fertiliser, and Gentoo Penguins improve some pastures by destroying diddle-dee when nesting.

Tussock-grass is the tallest native plant. Lt. Governor Moody, writing in 1842, stated '. . . by far the greater part of the coasts of these islands are fringed with it in many places to the breadth of half a mile; all the smaller islands are completely covered with it.' (*F. Is. Journal* 1969)

The acreage of tussock-grass is now much reduced and it occurs in its former abundance on only a few offshore islands. Most of these have suffered

20

interference from man. Many were burnt out accidentally or deliberately by sealers trying to evict the seals. Horses, sheep, cattle or pigs have been kept on most islands at some time, and large quantities of grass were cut for fodder when horses were more numerous. On Kidney Island, East Falkland (about 80 acres) the grass was regularly cut in the past and now, generally reaches a height of 8 to 10 ft. On Beauchêne Island (about 400 acres), the most isolated in the Falkland group, it reaches 15 ft. in places. (D.O.S. Survey party, 1959)

Several factors contribute to the dominance of mature tussock-grass (Figure 1). The height and close proximity of adjacent plants exclude most sunlight from the ground. The litter of tough dead stems falling from the 'skirt' of each clump is spread thickly over the ground by penguins, petrels and sea lions. Burrowing by Magellanic Penguins and petrels aerates the soil, and they deposit faeces rich in nitrogen beneath the plants. Where clearings have been made wild celery will flourish.

Kidney Island has a 90% cover of mature tussock-grass, in striking contrast to the Hard and Soft Camp on the mainland only half a mile away. A survey of the breeding birds, carried out over several seasons, showed that twenty-eight

Old bull Sea Lion resting on wild celery and tussock-grass.

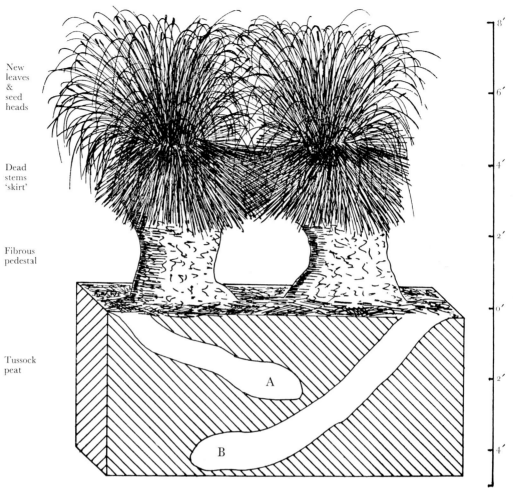

New
leaves
&
seed
heads

Dead
stems
'skirt'

Fibrous
pedestal

Tussock
peat

FIG. I. TUSSOCK-GRASS PROFILE.
DIAGRAMMATIC BURROWS OF: A. SHEARWATERS/SHOEMAKER; B. MAGELLANIC PENGUIN.

bird species bred on Kidney Island. This tussock-grass community provides abundant nest-sites and shelter from the wind for a surprising variety of birds, ranging in size from the Marsh Wren to the Turkey Vulture, and including five species of petrel.

Figure 2 shows diagrammatically the stratification of nest-sites of the seventeen species that nest on, in or under mature tussock-grass. Nine other species, including gulls, the Crested Caracara and Skua, use tussock-grass as nest material. The Brown-hooded Gull nests on Kidney Island, but only in low tussock-grass on a narrow rock outlier. The Black Oystercatcher is the only breeding species on Kidney Island that does not use tussock-grass in any way.

Sea-lions flatten some of the tops of tussock clumps on which they rest. The

22

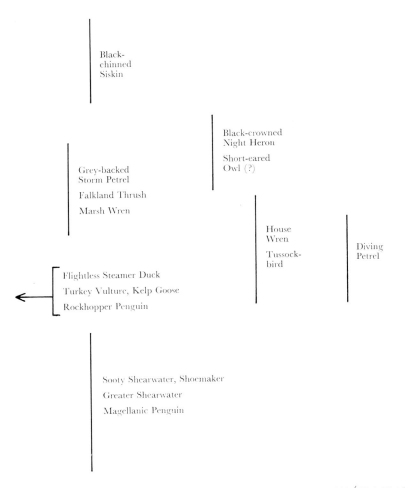

Black-
chinned
Siskin

Black-crowned
Night Heron

Short-eared
Owl (?)

Grey-backed
Storm Petrel

Falkland Thrush

Marsh Wren

House
Wren

Tussock-
bird

Diving
Petrel

Flightless Steamer Duck

Turkey Vulture, Kelp Goose

Rockhopper Penguin

Sooty Shearwater, Shoemaker

Greater Shearwater

Magellanic Penguin

FIG. 2. VERTICAL ZONATION OF NESTING-SITES IN TUSSOCK-GRASS (POA FLABELLATA)

remains of Grey-backed Storm-Petrels, Diving Petrels and owl pellets have been found here, and it is obvious that the flattened clumps are used as plucking sites by the Short-eared Owl. This is an interesting example of the inter-relationship between plant, mammal and bird.

It is remarkable enough that twenty-eight species nest on an island only three-quarters of a mile long and at the most about a quarter of a mile wide. When the *numbers* of each species are considered, the importance of tussock-grass becomes even more apparent.

At least 3,000 pairs of Rockhopper Penguins bred on Kidney Island in 1960; they shared the northern cliffs with 440 pairs of King Cormorants, 134 pairs of Rock Cormorants, about 50 pairs of South American Terns, 50 pairs of Dolphin

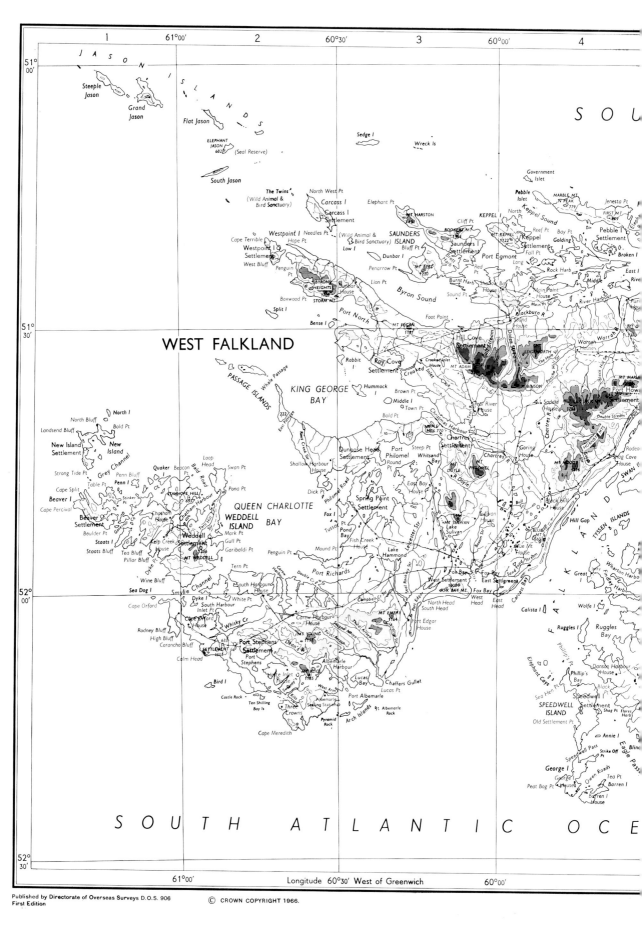

FALKLAND ISLANDS

SOUTH ATLANTIC OCEAN

EAST FALKLAND

LAFONIA

| Land over 2000 feet |
| 1500-2000 " |
| 1000-1500 " |
| 500-1000 " |
| below 500 " |

Heights in feet

Scale 1: 643,000

Miles 5   0   5   10   15   20 Miles

Roads _____
Tracks _____
Telephone Lines _____
Lighthouse, Beacon _____ ⚓ ·Bn

ALL TERRITORIAL WATERS ARE SEAL RESERVES

Beauchêne I
Whirlwind

(Seal Reserve,
Wild Animal &
Bird Sanctuary)

59°13'   59°10'
52°53'
52°56'

STANLEY

Compiled and drawn by Directorate of Overseas Surveys.

The hut on Kidney Island sheltered by tussock-grass.

Gulls and 20 pairs of Brown-hooded Gulls. The low rocky bays and southern coast were occupied by 14 pairs of Kelp Geese, 10 pairs of Flightless Steamer Ducks, 8 pairs of Night Herons and 5 pairs of Black Oystercatchers.

A significant proportion of the bird population nested below ground level. In places the peat was so riddled with burrows of Sooty Shearwaters, Shoemakers and Magellanic Penguins that it was likely to cave in underfoot. At night the air was filled with the eerie screams and howls of the petrels as they returned to their burrows.

Six of the nine Falkland passerines bred on Kidney Island. The Tussock-bird was the most numerous; thirty were once trapped and banded in four days near the hut. The Falkland Thrush here attained a population density higher than at any place on the adjacent mainland.

Kidney Island is fortunate in having a rich invertebrate fauna, including Camel-crickets, beetles and spiders in the grass and amphipods in rotting kelp

Southern Sea Lions on a boulder beach.

on the beach. It is also free of mammalian predators. It is not known whether the former coastal fringes of tussock-grass supported such a high density of birds, but it is obvious that there is every reason for protecting existing tussock-grass and for reinstating it wherever possible. (Colour photos: p. 192)

Changes in vegetation are difficult to assess, though there is no doubt that the appearance of the land has altered considerably since settlement began. Little early information is available. A few visitors and settlers reported incidentally on the vegetation. They noted the 'extensive plains of fine grassland' and there is a description of people walking with difficulty through 'a kind of hay a foot or so high which reached to the top of the mountains'. We are told that 'broom' (Fachine), diddle-dee and balsam bog were tried for fuel before peat was found. Some were intrigued by the tussock-grass 'like groves of low trees fringing the Islands' (M. B. R. Cawkell, 1960).

One can only guess at the extent of each plant species in early days. It was certainly excellent pasture land. Moody estimated that 30,000 fine, long-horned cattle and 3,000 wild horses roamed the Islands in 1842. These were the descendants of livestock introduced by early French settlers. The cattle were hunted extensively and exterminated by the 1880s, despite belated government attempts to protect them.

The following description of vegetation late in the 19th century was written by H. Felton.

'The northern part of the West Falkland from Chartres through Roy Cove and Hill Cove to White Rock was covered with grass bogs reaching to the rider's knees, interspersed with fine grass and acres of [wild] celery. In many places because of the growth, the camp was difficult to get through. Cattle were magnificent, enormously fat and very plentiful. This wealth of good fodder was destroyed during the fine summer of 1871 when it was fired, and the camp was burnt to the soil from Chartres to Port Purvis. It took fifteen years before there was a semblance of recovery, the [mountain] blue grass was pulled up by the sheep as soon as it started to grow, making the camp look like a hay field. Before this, stock kept fat summer and winter.' (Quoted in the *Falkland Islands Monthly Review* of 6th May 1963.)

It is interesting to note here, that sheep were established on East Falkland in 1852 and the first flocks of sheep were introduced to West Falkland in 1867. By 1870 there were 64,675 sheep in the Falklands; numbers reached a peak of 807,211 in 1898 (M. B. R. Cawkell). Sheep-farming, until recently, has been purely extractive and the pastures have deteriorated alarmingly on the main islands. Apart from the tussock-grass areas, the Hard Camp originally produced the best grazing for livestock, but continuous, largely uncontrolled grazing by sheep over the past century has seriously depleted many of the most palatable and nutritious grasses. Similarly, the shrubs Fachine on both main islands, and Box on West Falkland, have declined so that they now occur only in places inaccessible to sheep, such as steep sides of valleys and on sheltered cliffs. The disappearance of these shrubs and grasses must have seriously affected populations of birds.

Two birds that have suffered excessive predation by man since the peak of the sheep-farming era, are the Upland and Ruddy-headed Geese. Before sheep-farming started the 'Upland' geese were found, according to Darwin, 'throughout the interior of the island [East Falkland] rarely or never on the sea-coast and seldom even near fresh-water lakes'. The wide distribution of geese inland was presumably linked with an equally wide distribution of fine grasses. They certainly congregate in valleys and coastal areas today.

After sheep were introduced and became numerous, grassland was reduced to shorter turf in many places. This would have made more pasture suitable for geese and probably led to their increase. The same situation arose in Tierra del Fuego when sheep-farming became well established. Crawshay reported (1904) that even though many goose eggs were collected for winter use, partially incubated eggs destroyed and many young birds killed when flightless, both species of geese were still increasing markedly in Tierra del Fuego. At the same time, farmers in the Falklands became worried about the large numbers of geese because pastures showed signs of deterioration. The farmers variously said—without scientific proof—that four, five or seven geese ate as much grass as one sheep. An Ordinance was therefore passed in 1905 which provided for payment by Government, at a rate of ten shillings per hundred, for a nominal 25,000 beaks each from East and West Falkland in the first year. The total killed since that time must be hundreds of thousands. Payment by Government ceased some years ago, but several farms still pay a bounty for beaks.

Sheep have continued their selective free-ranging grazing in many areas and much good grass has disappeared. During the first quarter of this century the number of sheep fell by about 20%. Since then the total has remained relatively static, while the controversy over geese and pastures continues.

The geese are doubly unfortunate in being shot as vermin and as game for the table. Large flocks are sometimes rounded up, when the adults are moulting and the young not yet flying. They are clubbed to death and the beaks are taken. Many newly-laid eggs are taken for food and 'bad' (partially incubated) eggs are smashed. That both species are still to be seen in fair numbers can only be attributed to the small, widely scattered human population. The ecology of the Upland and Ruddy-headed Goose and their effect on pastures, certainly needs to be investigated.

Geese, in common with all ground-nesting birds, must have suffered from burning of the Camp. Intentional grass-burning was a well-established practice on many farms because it was thought to improve the pastures. The aim was to clear areas of rank White grass and allow sheep to graze the new green shoots. In fact, when grazing is allowed too soon after burning, the surface of the ground is broken up and any nutritious plants that have survived the burning are eaten out. This has led to much soil erosion.

The Falkland pastures have been surveyed by several grassland specialists during the past fifty years, and all have condemned the practice of grass-burning. It still continues, though on a much smaller scale. The specialists have strongly recommended subdivision of pastures by fences, which would allow land to be rested, improved or grazed in turn. Little pasture improvement has been attempted, compared with the size of the area suffering from over-grazing and the vast increase of unpalatable plants. There is a shortage of manpower for extra work, and the very high cost of importing fertilisers and fencing materials is prohibitive. Some farmers have ploughed or rotavated diddle-dee covered ground and followed this by sowing Yorkshire Fog, a grass which grows well in Falkland soils.

For a considerable time on West Point Island, the Napier family have been improving pastures by replanting former tussock-grass paddocks with thousands of small plants. Roddy Napier mentioned 30,000 in a period of thirty-five years. Losses due to gales and heavy rain have been high some years, but the results are most worthwhile especially in the more sheltered areas that were first replanted. Cinnamon grass has also been replanted there, even on a windswept slope 1,000 ft. above sea level. This plant is said to provide the favourite nesting habitat for the Short-eared Owl. (Colour photo: p. 207)

In the *Falkland Islands Journal* (1968) Mrs. Kitty Bertrand describes the pasture improvement work of Jason Hansen on Carcass Island.

'Unfortunately none of the early pioneers realised the value of the native tussac [or tussock-grass] for food and shelter, nor that it could only be stocked in the winter months. Consequently, Carcass lost nearly all of its valuable tussac border before anyone realised how to save it. ... [In 1927] there was only one tussac paddock (the Wreck), in use. Two others which had been fenced in, the Jetty Point and the Needles Point, had had their fences broken and during the summer stock destroyed them. The N.W. Point was a wilderness of sand and clay and black tussac soil. ...

'Mr. Hansen had early realised the importance of winter food and shelter ... He started by repairing the fences of the Jetty Point and Needles Point and resting them until the tussac grew up again.

'He then fenced the North West Point and, as there was nothing growing there, started the stupendous task of planting it with tussac and sand grass roots. The roots for this came from the Wreck paddock, the little island in Carcass Harbour and the Twins. The overland transport was by pack-horse or horse and cart. Roots about the thickness that a man could grasp easily in one hand were dibbed in row after row: thousands upon thousands of them with no mechanical means whatsoever: with only two men to help, year after year until all those acres were planted. Then he rested it for several years. The same procedure was followed with the Dyke Paddock, Gothic Point, the Rocky

Ridge Paddock and the West Paddock. The seed from the tussac was ineffective while the soil was still at the drifting stage. . . .

'By the late 1940's all sheep with the exception of the old wethers were wintered in tussac paddocks. The breeding ewes from May until the end of August and the rest from June until some time in September, the exact date when they are taken out depending on the wetness or dryness of the season.

'In 1955, we, the present owners [C. & K. Bertrand] sub-divided two camps, which thanks to Mr. Hansen's tussac paddocks for winter food and shelter, enabled us to practise rotational grazing successfully. By broadcasting Brown top and Yorkshire Fog seed in conjunction with the rotational grazing we have improved the grass land. . . .

'Mr. Hansen had two other great interests besides the improvement of the land, namely growing trees and the conservation of wild life. . . . Carcass Island has been virtually a wild life sanctuary since Mr. Jason Hansen owned it and we have endeavoured to continue his policy. . . . There being no rats, mice nor feral cats, most of the species of small birds breed on Carcass in considerable numbers. . . .

'The acreage of Carcass Island is 4,200, it carries on an average 2,200 sheep and approximately 20 cattle. There are now 25 miles of fencing on it, excluding settlement paddocks. Two more tussac paddocks and several more sub-divisions of other grassland are planned for the future.'

In terms of wool production per acre, Carcass Island is one of the foremost farms in the Falklands. The success of Carcass Island as a sheep farm demonstrates that the interests of man and the wild life are not in conflict, when a policy of fencing, pasture improvement and replanting of tussock-grass paddocks is being pursued.

FALKLAND BIRDS

Classification and Distribution of Breeding Birds

Birds constitute the class Aves in the animal kingdom and the birds of a definable area may be termed the avifauna. The avifauna of the Falkland Islands includes rather few breeding species, some of which are present in very large numbers concentrated round the coasts and on the smaller islands. Bird density inland, away from ponds or streams, is very low indeed.

Order, family, genus and species are terms used in biological classification.

An *order* consists of a number of families considered to have certain general affinities.

A *family* comprises few or many genera (plural of genus) with several recognizable similarities that separate them from other families.

A *genus* is a group of species considered to be closely related and with many basic characteristics in common.

A *species* is regarded as a biological unit, and is characterized by inherent reproductive isolation, i.e. two species inhabiting the same area do not normally interbreed.

A species may be sub-divided into geographical races (subspecies). The Kelp goose *Chloëphaga hybrida* for example, occurs in the Falklands, southern Chile and southern Argentina. The *Falkland Island* Kelp goose is larger than the continental bird and has therefore been classified as a race and given the additional subspecific name *malvinarum*; its full scientific name is *Chloëphaga hybrida malvinarum*.

Two further examples may help to clarify this scientific classification. The order PASSERIFORMES (passerines) comprises more than half of all the species of birds in the world, and more than a third of the recognized families. One of the families, Furnariidae (Ovenbirds), comprises 58 genera with about 221 species in South America, including Spinetails, Earthcreepers, Treerunners, etc. Only one species of the family Furnariidae, the Tussock-bird or Blackish Cinclodes is present in the Falkland Islands. In the Falklands there are two species of oystercatcher, *Haematopus leucopodus* and *H. ater*, belonging to the same genus, *Haematopus*, the only genus in the family Haematopodidae. This family is part of the order CHARADRIIFORMES, which includes among others, the families Charadriidae, Scolopacidae, Stercorariidae and Laridae.

The table opposite lists all fifty-nine known breeding species, including the House Sparrow in the family Ploceidae, which was introduced in the 1920s.

It can be seen that the breeding birds of the Falkland Islands are representative of 10 orders and 26 families. Only 17 species can be called true land birds, while 42 species depend on a fresh or salt water environment for food or refuge. Thus it can be inferred that although the Falkland Islands provide rather poor habitats for land birds, they have good habitats for water birds. The family with most genera and species in the Falklands is that of the Anatidae, which has 1 swan, 4 sheldgeese and 8 ducks. These are followed by the Procellariidae (petrels and shearwaters) and the Spheniscidae (penguins). Few representatives of passerine families with many species in South America have been able to adapt themselves to the windy and exposed habitats of the Falklands. Argentina has about 436 species of passerines while the Falklands can support only 9 native species.

TABLE I. *Classification of Falkland Islands Breeding Birds*

Order	Family	Genera	Species
SPHENISCIFORMES	Spheniscidae—Penguins	4	5
PODICIPEDIFORMES	Podicipedidae—Grebes	1	2
PROCELLARIIFORMES	Diomedeidae—Albatrosses	1	1
	Procellariidae—Petrels and Shearwaters	4	6
	Hydrobatidae—Storm-Petrels	2	2
	Pelecanoididae—Diving Petrels	1	1
PELECANIFORMES	Phalacrocoracidae—Cormorants	1	2
CICONIIFORMES	Ardeidae—Herons	1	1
ANSERIFORMES	Anatidae—Sheldgeese, Swans and Ducks	5	13
FALCONIFORMES	Cathartidae—New World Vultures	1	1
	Accipitridae—Hawks	1	1
	Falconidae—Falcons and Caracaras	3	3
CHARADRIIFORMES	Haematopodidae—Oystercatchers	1	2
	Charadriidae—Plovers	2	2
	Scolopacidae—Snipe	1	1
	Stercorariidae—Skuas	1	1
	Laridae—Gulls and Terns	3	4
STRIGIFORMES	Strigidae—Owls	1	1
PASSERIFORMES	Furnariidae—Ovenbirds	1	1
	Tyrannidae—Tyrant Flycatchers	1	1
	Troglodytidae—Wrens	2	2
	Turdidae—Thrushes	1	1
	Motacillidae—Pipits	1	1
	Icteridae—Meadowlarks	1	1
	Fringillidae—Finches	2	2
	Ploceidae—Weaverbirds	1	1

Non-breeding migrants include seven species which breed in the Antarctic and are seen during the winter. The other two species are North American waders which are present during the Falkland summer. All occur regularly in their non-breeding seasons.

Vagrants from South America or the Antarctic are more than half of the species of birds recorded in the Falklands. The species that occur most frequently are small passerines, such as birds of the swallow family, several species in the heron family, a dove, a coot and a plover. All these breed in Patagonia or Tierra del Fuego except the Barn Swallow, which breeds in North America and regularly migrates to southern South America.

It is easy to understand how birds could be blown towards the Falklands in the prevailing westerlies. Many more species obviously reach the Falklands but

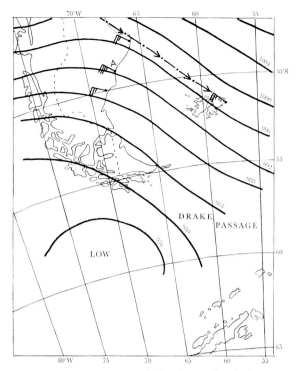

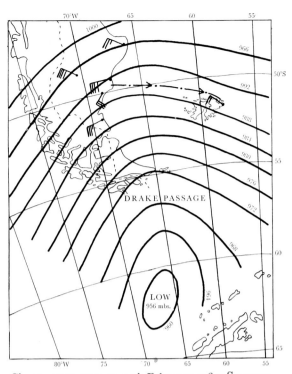

Chart 1. 1800 GMT. on 7th October 1960: Spring.

Chart 2. 1200 GMT. on 14th February 1960: Summer.

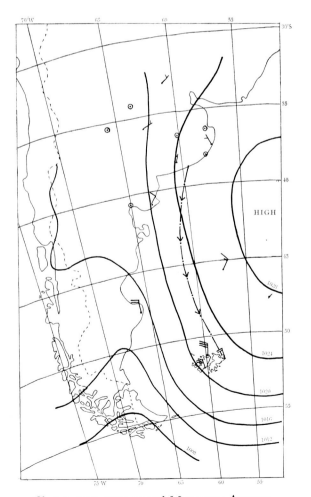

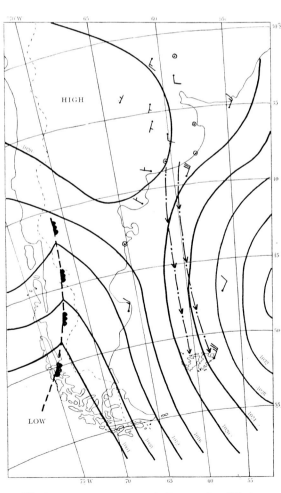

Chart 3. 1200 GMT. on 3rd May 1957: Autumn.

Chart 4. 1200 GMT. on 13th June 1960: Winter.

FIG. 3. 'VAGRANT-SITUATION' METEOROLOGICAL CHARTS

The four charts reproduced have lines of equal atmospheric pressure (isobars) drawn at 4 millibar intervals. Observations of the direction and strength of the wind at Argentine and Falkland stations are shown by one-sided arrows that point towards the stations. Each full barb represents 10 knots and each half barb represents 5 knots; e.g. on Chart 1., station 'A' had a NW'ly wind of 35 knots. Calm conditions are shown by a circle round the station point. Possible routes taken by the vagrant birds are shown by the lines with arrows.

Chart 1. 1800 GMT. on 7th October 1960: Spring.

A low pressure area was moving eastward through Drake Passage. Strong to gale force NW'ly winds extended from southern Argentina across the Falklands. A Barn Swallow was first seen in Stanley at 2100 GMT. on 7th October.

Chart 2. 1200 GMT. on 14th February 1960: Summer.

An intense depression was moving northeastward near the South Shetland Islands. SW to W'ly gales were blowing across Patagonia and W'ly gale force winds towards the Falklands. An Eared Dove probably reached Port Louis, East Falkland, on this day, where it survived for three weeks until it was killed by a cat.

Chart 3. 1200 GMT. on 3rd May 1957: Autumn.

An anticyclone which had developed over Buenos Aires Province, Argentina, was drifting rapidly southeastward. Strong N'ly winds covered part of the South Atlantic from eastern Argentina to the Falklands. A Snowy Egret hit Cape Pembroke lighthouse, during that night.

Chart 4. 1200 GMT. on 13th June 1960: Winter.

Anticyclones north and east of the Falklands and a warm front moving across the Andes towards Patagonia, produced strong NE'ly winds from the mouth of the River Plate to the Falklands. A Striated Heron was found at Carcass Island in mid-June and a Purple Gallinule was killed by a cat at Port Louis at about the same time.

are not seen. Some birds may be noticed because they are conspicuous or have noisy calls, like the Common Egret, Chilean Lapwing or Buff-necked Ibis. Small birds that depend on flying insects like the Chilean Swallow and Barn Swallow, are often attracted to Stanley and Camp settlements where blow-flies are common. Sometimes it is possible to estimate the route a vagrant has taken from the South American mainland by studying the current meteorological charts. Some examples of typical 'vagrant-situations' are reproduced on p. 34 with notes on the particular species recorded.

People have been living in the Falkland Islands for little more than two hundred years. The first recorded landing was made in 1690. Settlement was intermittent from 1764 to 1831 and has been continuous since 1833. The capital town of Stanley was established in 1843 because of the excellent inner and outer harbours of Port William. The total population is now about 2,000, of whom half live in Stanley on the east coast of East Falkland. The population density for the Falkland Islands excluding Stanley, is approximately one person to every 4·7 square miles. When it is realized that most of the other 1,000 people live in widely scattered, coastal settlements, it is obvious that much of the land can be termed uninhabited. In many areas little is known of the bird life.

Although there are reports that vast numbers of birds were seen by the early settlers in the 18th century, there is little information about individual species. Few ornithologists have written about the birds of the Falklands. The oldest reliable records were made by Charles Darwin during his voyage on H.M.S. *Beagle*. His brief visits, each of about a month, were in March and April 1833 and 1834. Possibly the most interesting of the twenty species he noted was the Striated Caracara, which was then very numerous on East and West Falkland and was remarkably tame for a bird of prey. The first ornithologist resident in the Falklands was Captain C. C. Abbott, who spent at least three years in Stanley and published notes on sixty-six species in 1861.

R. Vallentin made three visits to the Falklands between 1898 and 1911, during which he lived in Stanley and at Shallow Bay, West Falkland. He contributed a chapter containing many interesting observations to V. F. Boyson's book, *The Falkland Islands* (1924). W. S. Brooks and R. H. Beck, who were both collecting for American museums, each spent five months in the Falklands between October 1915 and February 1916. Brooks lists forty-two species from Stanley, San Carlos and Port Stephens (1917). Beck collected and photographed birds in the Stanley area, on Kidney, Cochon, Bleaker and West Point Islands. An account of his work is given in Murphy's *Oceanic Birds of South America* (1936).

Two first-year Striated Caracaras from West Point Island.

In 1926, A. G. Bennett, who was a resident of Stanley for thirty years, published a comprehensive list of 102 Falkland birds. This followed a list in Spanish published in the journal *El Hornero* in 1921, by R. Wace. Bennett's list contained several additional species and notes on specimens collected in the Falkland Islands Dependencies; it remained current for thirty-five years. Bennett was a keen collector and amateur taxidermist, who put his collecting to good use by establishing a fine display of birds in the Stanley Museum. Unfortunately, nearly all his carefully mounted specimens were lost in 1945, when the old Town Hall was destroyed by fire.

An interesting small book published in 1933, was written by A. F. Cobb, who was a farmer on Bleaker Island when R. H. Beck visited that island in 1915. It was entitled *Birds of the Falkland Islands* and contained notes on thirty species, most of which were illustrated with his own photographs.

J. E. Hamilton, who was a Government Naturalist studying seals for many years, published several notes on Falkland birds between 1934 and 1954. In 1950, Hamilton and G. Hattersley-Smith reported on a plentiful deposit of bird bones found preserved under 9 ft. of peat on West Point Island. These provide the earliest evidence we have of Striated Caracara, Black-throated Finch, Common Snipe and penguins in the Falklands, and they are worthy of further investigation.

In 1960, E. M. Cawkell, who spent five years in the Falklands (1950–5), contributed a chapter on 'Bird Life' to *The Falkland Islands* (Cawkell, Maling & Cawkell). In 1961 he published the latest annotated list of Falkland birds, incorporating the notes of Hamilton, who had died in 1957. They noted a total of 126 species and included many valuable records of distribution and breeding behaviour. O. S. Pettingill jr. has published several papers on Falkland birds following his visits in 1953/4 and 1971/2, the most recent being a detailed paper on the nine native passerines, which appeared in 1973. Notes from the records of these ornithologists have been mentioned or discussed in the text where they are appropriate.

It is unfortunate that most of man's activities concerning birds in the Falkland Islands have not been in pursuit of knowledge.

Penguins are among the most popular families of birds today, yet King, Gentoo, Rockhopper and Magellanic Penguins have been victimized in the Falkland Islands for at least two centuries. Millions were tried out for their oil, and breeding populations of all these species suffered terrible losses from late in the

18th century, when seal-hunting started in the Falklands. The King Penguin, which became temporarily extinct in the Falklands, was killed for its beautiful skin as well as for oil. Murphy (1936) quotes a report published by Sclater in 1868: 'In 1857 four small schooners at the Falklands tried out 50,700 gallons (230,480 litres) of penguin oil, implying the slaughter of nearly half a million birds during a single season.' Brooks (1917) states that, 'Schooners used to visit colonies in spring and autumn, set up try-pots and corrals into which birds were driven in thousands and clubbed. A penguin furnished about one pint of oil, a gallon of which brought two shillings and sixpence. A sea-captain in this business for years said his vessel annually destroyed about 70,000 birds.' The practice of trying-out penguins ceased about 1871, when New England sealers stopped visiting the Falklands. Incidentally, Brooks also reported that the snowy breasts of male Kelp Geese were sold in considerable numbers in London, until this traffic became illegal (probably under the Importation of Plumage (Prohibition) Act of 1921).

Eggs of all four species of penguin have been taken for food since men reached the Falklands. The Gentoo Penguin can apparently compensate for this by repeated layings without appreciably decreasing the number of young produced (Murphy, 1936). The Rockhopper Penguin is not so resilient, and several colonies have declined or disappeared within living memory. In 1871 a colony of Rockhoppers at Sparrow Cove near Stanley, yielded 25,000 eggs, but none breed there today. Another colony, on Kidney Island, produced 25,000 eggs in 1914, but only 1,000 in 1952, though this colony is easily accessible and all eggs could have been taken. Few eggs have been collected on Kidney Island since, and the colony numbered about 3,000 pairs in 1960. Since this island was declared a Nature Reserve in 1964, they should now breed there undisturbed. Penguin eggs are still gathered for food under licence, for which the Government charges a nominal sum. The Magellanic Penguin has suffered less than the other species because it nests in deep burrows and the eggs are comparatively difficult to collect.

Three birds of prey were classified as vermin in 1908, when an Ordinance authorized the payment of four pence for each Turkey Vulture beak and two pence for each beak of the Crested Caracara and Striated Caracara. The bounty per beak has risen since then and the destruction continues, except in the case of the Striated Caracara. This species was given official protection in the 1920s after agitation by J. E. Hamilton, yet it was still being shot as late as 1963 on the Jason Islands. In the years from 1953 to 1959, between £7 and £47 was paid annually by Government as bounties for the 'Destruction of Birds of Prey'.

Some farmers do not support this destruction, but others allege that these birds of prey, and the Giant Petrel, Kelp Gull and Great Skua, do appreciable damage to cast sheep and young lambs. It can be argued that these scavenging birds perform a useful service for the farmers by clearing thousands of unwanted carcasses from the Camp. The Kelp Gull and Skua are both known to kill goslings, and could act as a natural control on the numbers of Upland and Ruddy-headed Geese.

Apart from the Upland and Ruddy-headed Geese, several other species are shot for sport. Unfortunately, many people who shoot cannot distinguish between protected and unprotected birds. These people are mainly visitors from ships or short-stay residents. Nominally protected species which have been shot or otherwise killed include Ashy-headed Goose, Kelp Goose, Flightless Steamer Duck, Red-backed Hawk, Cinereous Harrier, Striated Caracara, Peregrine Falcon and Rufous-chested Dotterel.

All mammalian predators now living in the Falklands were introduced deliberately or accidentally by man. These are domestic cats, Brown rats, House mice and Silver foxes, the latter from Patagonia. The only native terrestrial mammal was the Falkland Island Fox or Wolf, known as a 'Warrah' to the early settlers. This fox was reported to be absurdly tame and fearless of man, and it lived on young seals, birds and eggs before sheep were introduced. By 1876 it was exterminated, because it was considered to be a menace to sheep.

Cats do considerable damage near settlements to passerine species such as the Falkland Thrush and Dark-faced Ground-tyrant. Some cats are semi-wild and some feral cats live in the open Camp, where they must take small birds and mice. Many cats were introduced to New Island to kill Slender-billed Prions, because their burrowing activities were said to make the ground unsafe for horses. Fortunately, they have had little effect on the prions, which still breed there in thousands. West Point Island has some breeding prions, and several nest-burrows examined in March 1962 contained the chewed remains of full-grown birds. This appeared to be the work of rats, which are known to have colonized several islands and parts of East and West Falkland from wrecked sailing ships. Where they have become established, rats compete seriously with passerines and petrels.

House mice can also be found living wild in the Camp away from settlements. They probably live on seeds and berries and do little harm to birds, but they are known to be partly carnivorous and have been seen feeding on sheep carcasses (E. M. Cawkell, 1960). They may also take eggs of small birds.

Silver foxes were introduced to some far western islands, probably early this century. Staats Island, near Weddell Island, has a large population, which apparently preys on Magellanic Penguins and their eggs. Staats Island also had a thriving colony of the herbivorous Guanaco, which was introduced from Patagonia. This animal would have an indirect effect by reducing vegetational cover for land-birds.

Interest in the conservation of wild life in the Falkland Islands has developed steadily in recent years. A radically revised Wild Animals and Birds Protection Ordinance was enacted in 1964, and a Nature Reserves Ordinance became law in the same year.

The Wild Animals and Birds Protection Ordinance gives protection through-out the year to most Falkland Island birds. Two categories of birds, pests and game-birds, are excluded or partly excluded. Eight species are regarded as pests and may be killed at any time. These are: Slender-billed Prion, Ruddy-headed Goose, Upland Goose, Turkey Vulture, Crested Caracara, Great Skua, Kelp Gull and House Sparrow. Five other species are classified as game-birds and may only be killed outside the Close Season, which extends from the first day of August to the last day of the following February, inclusive. These species are: Patagonian Crested Duck, Speckled Teal, Chiloë Wigeon, Silver Teal and Common Snipe.

This Ordinance is a great improvement on its predecessor; nevertheless, several points can be criticized. A notable omission is any form of protection for the eggs of wild birds other than those of penguins and the Black-browed Albatross, which can only be taken under licence. It is illogical to give implicit protection to certain rare species of birds and yet allow their eggs to be taken.

The ecology of all species listed as pests, should be studied in order to deter-mine whether they affect the sheep-farming industry in any way.

It is regrettable that pole and gin traps are considered lawful means of killing Turkey Vultures and Crested Caracaras. Both types of trap should be banned because their use endangers all other birds of prey.

A most valuable section of this Ordinance allowed for the establishment of wild animal or bird sanctuaries on Crown lands, in Colonial waters or, with the consent of the owner or lessee, on private land. Within sanctuaries, all wild life is protected, no grazing or carnivorous animals may be introduced and access

Bull Elephant Seal moulting on deep sand at Volunteer Lagoon.

is restricted. Under this Ordinance, several sanctuaries have been declared. Beauchêne Island, Low Island and The Twins were the first on 30th December 1964. Beauchêne Island supports the largest breeding colony of Black-browed Albatrosses in the Falklands, while Low Island and The Twins are small, privately owned, tussock islands northwest of West Falkland. Middle Island in King George Bay was declared a sanctuary on 19th July 1966, followed in 1968 by the first two areas on East Falkland, Cape Dolphin and the coastal region from Cow Bay to Volunteer Point.

Northern cliffs of Kidney Island looking westward to Cochon Island.

The Nature Reserves Ordinance authorises the declaration of Nature Reserves on which hunting, egg-collecting and burning or cutting of vegetation are prohibited. Public access and movement within Nature Reserves can also be restricted. The first Nature Reserves to be declared in the Falkland Islands were Kidney Island and Cochon Island in Berkeley Sound. Both became Reserves in 1964. Bird Island, off Port Stephens was declared a Nature Reserve in 1969.

Section two of the Nature Reserves Ordinance states: 'In this Ordinance "nature reserve" means land reserved for the purpose of protecting, and of providing, under suitable conditions and control, special opportunities for the study of, and research into, matters relating to the flora and fauna of the Colony.' It is essential that a thorough ecological study of the Nature Reserves is undertaken, if the Colony is to benefit fully from these protected areas of plant and animal life.

The interest taken in the Islands by tourists is a further encouraging sign for wild life. The first Antarctic tourist cruise in 1968 brought Mr. Len Hill to the Falklands. He subsequently bought Grand and Steeple Jason Islands and has established them as sanctuaries. These two islands have large seabird colonies and are among the few remaining strongholds of the Striated Caracara.

The history of man's occupation of the Falklands is largely one of extraction and destruction of the natural resources. Millions of birds and animals have been killed for gain, or even exterminated; the vegetation has been depleted and the land impoverished. Cats, dogs, rats, mice, rabbits, hares, silver foxes, guanacos, sheep, cattle, pigs, horses and blowflies have been introduced within two centuries, and all are affecting the natural balance.

Life in the Falkland Islands is arduous, especially for those involved in farming, and the well-being of the human population must come first in any future developments. However, much more should be done to restore and improve the natural vegetation, so that increased productivity of the Islands is not won at the expense of the most attractive natural inhabitants, the Falkland Island birds.

Check List of Falkland Islands Birds

Key to abbreviations used in this list:

B   Breeding species
M   Migratory species
N   Non-breeding regular visitors
V   Vagrants recorded five or more times
A   Accidental visitors recorded less than five times
L   Lost breeding species
?   Status uncertain

47

Order FALCONIFORMES   Family Cathartidae

Family Accipitridae

Family Falconidae

Order GRUIFORMES   Family Rallidae

Order CHARADRIIFORMES   Family Haematopodidae

Key to Families of Falkland Islands Birds

This Key should enable an observer who has noticed some features of a bird (e.g. size, colour patterns, shape or size of bill, shape of the wings or relative length of neck and tail) to place it in one of the thirty-three families described in the Field Guide. Reference is given to the page on which the first representative of that family is described. In sixteen families only one species breeds or occurs regularly in the Falklands; therefore the Key also gives specific identification features for these sixteen species.

The Key functions by eliminating alternatives, and the observer should work through it from the beginning whenever a bird is to be identified. A useful aid to identification is the size of a bird from the tip of the bill to the tail tip. The following scale, devised by Fisher (1954) and adapted to Falkland birds, is used in the Key and the text.

Adjective	Length in inches	Example
Very minute	4–5	Grass Wren $4\frac{1}{2}''$
Minute	5–6	Black-chinned Siskin 5″
Very small	6–8	Two-banded Plover 7″
Small	8–12	Falkland Thrush 10″
Small-medium	12–16	Speckled Teal 15″
Medium	16–20	Magellanic Oystercatcher 17″
Medium-large	20–24	Kelp Gull 20–23″
Large	24–28	Turkey Vulture 26″
Very large	28–32	Gentoo Penguin 30″
Immense	32–36	Giant Petrel 33–36″
Gigantic	36+	Wandering Albatross 44–53″

1. a. Non-flying large to gigantic seabirds; walk upright and stand very erect; plumage mainly blue-grey or black above, white beneath; swim expertly underwater using flippers (modified wings); large heads and thick necks show when swimming on surface. Spheniscidae/Penguins (*p.* 67)

   b. Flying birds [*see* 2]

2. a. Very small to gigantic black-brown and white or grey seabirds with long, narrow wings; bills deeply grooved, markedly hooked, often bulbous-tipped, nostrils in external tube(s) above bill; pelagic outside breeding season [*see* 3]

   b. Very small to small; bill as in 2.a., but wings short and pointed; body dumpy, plumage black above, white below; feet blue; flight whirring near sea surface; dive frequently from flight and fly underwater: Pelecanoididae/Diving Petrels (*p.* 96)

   c. Not as above [*see* 4]

3. a. Very large to gigantic seabirds (wingspan 8–11 ft.); wings very long and narrow; expert fliers that glide and turn constantly, hardly flapping wings; bills very heavy, hook-tipped; heads large and rounded; tails mostly short, broad and square; often follow ships; feed from sea surface; underwing dark with white band down centre in commonest species: Diomedeidae/Albatrosses (*p.* 76)

   b. Small to immense seabirds with long, narrow wings (wingspan 3–7 ft.); typically alternate between flapping and gliding on stiff wings; bills thin and bulbous-tipped to very heavy, all hooked; mostly pelagic outside breeding-season: Procellariidae/Shearwaters, Petrels and Fulmars (*p.* 80)

   c. Very small black and white or grey seabirds with fluttering, dancing flight on rapidly beating wings; often tread water while flying; legs long and very slender; bills black, short and hooked: Hydrobatidae/Storm-Petrels (*p.* 93)

4. a. Medium-large to gigantic waterside birds with very long legs, long dagger-shaped bills and long necks which are folded back in flight giving a thick-chested appearance; wings broad and slow-flapping; feet project beyond tail in flight; feed by wading slowly and stabbing fish in shallows: Ardeidae/Herons (*p.* 103)

   b. Very large black and grey marsh and pasture birds with long, thin, down-curved black bill; broad long wings; fly with neck extended fully. One vagrant species irregularly occurring has orange neck and breast, black belly and primaries and dark red legs; call very loud and much used: Threskiornithidae/Ibises (*p.* 107)

    c. Small to gigantic, long-necked and web- or lobe-footed; mainly waterside, freshwater or seabirds that dabble, dive or graze; neck is extended in flight and feet are hidden [*see* 5]

    d. Not noticeably long-necked [*see* 6]

5. a. Small to small-medium round-bodied, 'tailless'; long, thin-necked waterbirds that dive frequently and rarely fly; mainly black; head peaked with distinctive pattern or pale 'ear-tufts' in summer; bills black and sharp-pointed; feet lobed: Podicipedidae/Grebes (*p.* 74)

    b. Large or very large, black and white (immatures dark brown) seabirds with slender, sinuous necks and long hooked bills; tail longish; wings broad; flight direct and steady with rapid wing-beats; dive frequently from low swimming position with long head and bill typically uptilted; sea and coastal cliffs: Phalacrocoracidae/Cormorants (*p.* 97)

    c. Small-medium to gigantic; bulky; bills broad and flattened with short legs *or* deep and short bills with longer legs; float high on water; all have medium to long thick necks and rounded heads carried horizontally; flight direct and powerful with necks extended; wings broad, sharp-pointed, mostly well-patterned with white; tails mostly short; feet hidden in flight; feed by dabbling, diving or grazing. One species has very heavy head, bill and body, very short wings and is incapable of free flight: Anatidae/Ducks, Geese and Swans (*p.* 108)

6. a. Very small to medium-large, fairly long-legged wading birds [*see* 7]

    b. Medium to medium-large sea and coastal birds with fairly long pointed wings, angled when gliding [*see* 8]

    c. Not long-billed *and* long-winged [*see* 9]

7. a. Medium to medium-large; black or black and white shorebirds with very long straight, heavy red bills; long pink legs; fly with quick and shallow beats of longish, pointed wings; calls loud and piercing, used much in flight: Haematopodidae/Oystercatchers (*p.* 142)

    b. Very small to small-medium, round-headed birds of shores and grassy slopes; bills slender, pointed, shorter than head; legs fairly long; run with horizontal carriage, stop and tilt whole body to pick up food; black or white head stripes or both; flight rapid, wings sharp-pointed (*or* rounded); tails dark with white sides (*or* basal half white and terminal half black): Charadriidae/Lapwings and Plovers (*p.* 147)

   c. Very small to small-medium wading birds of beaches, mudflats and marshes; bill as long as head to much longer, straight or slightly down-curved; legs fairly long; wings sharp-pointed often with whitish bar across secondaries; tail barred or dark with whitish sides, or with white rump; feed by probing or picking in mud or on sand; flight very rapid, erratic; flocks perform aerial evolutions: Scolopacidae/Snipe and Sand-pipers (*p.* 151)

8. a. Medium-large heavily built dark brown seabirds showing large white flash on primaries in flight; bill heavy, hooked, black; legs and feet black; flight powerful; wings broad and sharply pointed; tail short; wing-beats fairly rapid in shallow arc; agile in pursuit of other seabirds, forcing them to disgorge food: Stercorariidae/Skuas (*p.* 160)

   b. Small-medium to medium-large coastal seabirds with long, pointed narrow to broad wings, angled midway when gliding; wing-beats slow and deep flapping; tail square or forked; white or grey below, grey, black or white above (adults), mottled brown and white (immature); bill heavy, slightly hooked to slender and pointed; feed in coastal waters by dropping to surface or shallow plunge-diving; float very high when swimming; often in flocks especially in winter; two species scavenge around settlements: Laridae/Gulls and Terns (*p.* 162)

9. a. Long-winged birds of prey with short or stout strongly hooked bills [*see* 10]

   b. Bill not heavy and hooked [*see* 12]

10. a. Mainly nocturnal hunters with forward-facing eyes set in a facial disc [*see* 11]

   b. Large, all dark coloured with very broad, long, 'fingered' wings, small head and longish, graduated tail; slow flapping flight with typical wavering action and frequent gliding with wings held about 30° above horizontal; bill heavy, hooked, whitish: Cathartidae/Vultures (*p.* 129)

   c. Medium to medium-large; heavy rounded head and short, strongly hooked bill; broad, rounded 'fingered' wings; short, square tail, white or whitish with broad black tip; glide with wings nearly flat, also hover: Accipitridae/Hawks (*p.* 132)

d. Small to large diurnal birds of prey; two types—
   i. Small to medium; fast-flying; narrow, curved and pointed wings; longish tails; dark 'moustachial' stripes;
   ii. Medium-large to large, mainly dark brown; long and broad 'fingered' wings with large pale primary patch; long tail whitish with black bar *or* black with white tip; heavy, pale, hooked bill and bare facial skin; flight flapping and gliding; walk and run: Falconidae/i. Falcons, ii. Caracaras (*p.* 134)

11. a. Small-medium; orange-buff above, buff-white below or grey; white heart-shaped facial disc; bill strongly curved, short and hooked; legs fairly long covered with white feathers; flight slow, silent and wavering on broad, rounded wings; call an eerie scream: Tytonidae/Barn Owls (*p.* 175)
    b. Small to small-medium; brown barred and streaked heavily with black, buff or white; eyes large, set in rounded facial disc; bill short, strongly curved and hooked; legs feathered, long sharp claws; in flight look heavy headed, with long, broad and rounded wings; short tail: Strigidae/ Owls (*p.* 176)

12. a. Small-medium to medium, bulky, black 'tailless' water birds with short, thick necks and small heads; short, stout, pointed yellow bill with red or yellow frontal shield on forehead; large lobed feet set far back; dive frequently; flight low, looks weak; wings rather short; patter over surface to take off: Rallidae/Coots (*p.* 141)
    b. Short-billed, pigeon-like shore or land birds [*see* 13]
    c. Not pigeon-like *or* 'tailless' water birds [*see* 14]

13. a. Small, plump, round-headed; light brown above and below; short, thick reddish legs and short pointed bill; flight rapid on longish, pointed wings; tail fairly long, graduated and often fanned open in flight; ground-feeders, walk and pick in gardens: Columbidae/Doves (*p.* 175)
    b. Very small to small, plump; variegated above brown, rufous and black; breast and belly white; resemble game-bird (Partridge/Quail) on ground; bill short, stout and curved; legs very short; flight rapid and erratic on long, sharp-pointed wings (resembles Plover); *Th. rumicivorus* has short black tail with broad white tip: Thinocoridae/Seedsnipes (*p.* 158)
    c. All white, medium-sized, pigeon-like shorebird with short, stout, pale bill, stout blue-grey legs and bare skin below eye; walks and runs like

pigeon; in flight has quick and shallow wing-beats; head and tail look short; feeds by scavenging around seal and penguin colonies and on shores: Chionididae/Sheathbills (*p.* 159)

14. a. Small; all dark brown; rather long, slender and slightly down-curved black bill; black legs; restless, pugnacious and tame; runs rapidly; flight rapid, fast wing-beats and gliding, showing pale brown wing bar; calls high-pitched, trilling: Furnariidae/Cinclodes etc. (*p.* 180)

  b. Minute to small, long-winged flycatching birds, with fairly long tails [*see* 15]

  c. Not as a. or b. above [*see* 16]

15. a. Very small; slim, with upright stance; grey-brown above, whitish below with black patch around eye and brown crown; tail fairly long, black with white outer edges; long black legs; short pointed black bill; tail fanned and flicked and wings flicked frequently; flight swift and easy on rather long wings; can hover: Tyrannidae/Tyrant-flycatchers (*p.* 182)

  b. Minute to small; blackish *or* black and white/buff aerial flycatchers; medium to long pointed wings; longish, variably forked tails; flight rapid and agile, fluttering, gliding and swooping; rarely land on ground: Hirundinidae/Swallows and Martins (*p.* 184)

16. a. Small; black above and tail; brilliant crimson breast (duller on female and young); broad curving white eyestripe; rather long, conical and sharply-pointed whitish bill; runs with ungainly action and feeds on ground; in flight white underwing is prominent; crouches when perched: Icteridae/Meadowlarks (*p.* 196)

  b. Very minute to small; mainly brown and buff; *no* white outer tail-feathers [*see* 17]

  c. Not as above [*see* 18]

17. a. Small; robust; dark brown and black above; rich buff below (juveniles spotted with black below); bill stout, pointed, orange or brown; legs fairly long, orange-yellow; head variably blackish around eye; tail black, rump olive-grey; ground-feeder, hops, bounds and runs; flicks tail up on alighting; song monotonous peeping whistle delivered from high perches: Turdidae/Thrushes (*p.* 191)

  b. Very minute to minute; brown, streaked above *or* banded on wings and tail only; rotund body with thin tail often cocked up over back; very active and mouselike, creeping through vegetation; flight weak and slow on whirring, rounded wings; tame and inquisitive; loud variable songs: Troglodytidae/Wrens (*p.* 186)

    c. Very small; dull brown and grey; perky and plump; short, heavy conical bill; tail all brown; no yellow on wings; bold and noisy; lives close to man; male has white cheeks, black throat (bib), dark grey crown and brown nape: Ploceidae/Weaverfinches (*p.* 204)

    d. Minute; grey head with thick black stripes; broad chestnut collar across nape; throat white; breast and flanks grey; tail rather long, brown; flight jerky and undulating; back striated heavily buff and dark brown: Fringillidae (Emberizinae)/Buntings (*p.* 199)

18. a. Minute to very small; green or brown with marked yellow bars on tail or wings or both; bills short and conical; ground or bush feeders; calls squeaky; flocks in winter: Fringillidae/Finches and Buntings (*p.* 199)

    b. Very small; slender; heavily striated brown and buff above; tail brown with white sides; bill slender; hind toe long; flight jerky, undulating over long distances; song-flight: mounts to c100 ft. and parachutes down; ground-feeder; runs through grass: Motacillidae/Pipits (*p.* 195)

    c. Not as above; possibly vagrant species in a Family not included in this Key.

Explanatory Notes to Field Guide

Identification details are given for the eighty-seven species most likely to be seen in the Falkland Islands. These include all breeding species, all regular non-breeding visitors and those vagrants known to have occurred on at least five occasions. Records of all other vagrant species identified and notes on some former breeding species are included in the next section, 'Vagrants and Lost Breeding Species'.

The vernacular and scientific names used are those accepted in the American continent, which in some cases are different from those accepted in Britain. The order of species and nomenclature follow R. Meyer de Schaunsee's *A Guide to the Birds of South America* (1971), as it is the most recent comprehensive list. However, in a few cases it was considered justifiable to use subspecific vernacular names for clearly separable Falkland races.

'A' and 'C' indicate the Argentine and Chilean book-names respectively.

IDENTIFICATION. The following aids to identification are given: Relative size, for use with the Key to Families, approximate ('c' = circa/about) body-length in inches, measured from bill tip to tail tip. Wing-span is added where it aids identification in flight. Characters of each species as seen in the field are given, with the best identification marks and prominent plumage patterns in italics. Descriptions are included of plumage variations between male and female, adult and immature birds and between breeding and non-breeding plumage. Where there is no mention of differences between male and female, it can usually be assumed that they cannot be separated in the field. Additional notes on characteristic behaviour are added for most species.

VOICE. Descriptions of typical calls and their use are given, with differences from calls of related species. For birds that sing or produce special calls associated with the breeding-season, there is a description of the song, an indication of the song-period and the types of perches used.

FOOD. The main items of diet are given where they are known, as well as notes on the feeding methods of some birds.

HABITAT, STATUS & BREEDING. An indication of the relative abundance of each species in the Falkland Islands is given, i.e. whether it is common, fairly common, locally common or rare, with a description of the usual habitat, and whether it occupies a different habitat in the winter from that used in the breeding season. For migrants, an indication is given of the approximate arrival and departure dates with earliest and latest records. A description of the eggs, the number in each clutch, the nest-site and nest-materials is given for breeding species. Where the possibility is not mentioned of more than one brood being raised in a season, it is believed that the species is normally single-brooded. Estimations of breeding-seasons, distributions, etc., have been made on the basis of the information available in the published literature, from personal records and private communications.

Some figures of birds banded in the Falkland Islands between 1957 and 1965 are given, with information on longevity and movements resulting from the recovery of banded birds.

Non-breeding species and regular visitors have been discussed under an alternative heading to this section: ‘*Habitat, Status & Records*’. ‘*Voice*’ and ‘*Food*’ are omitted from the notes on most of the non-breeding species unless relevant to identification in the field.

DISTRIBUTION ABROAD. For South American land-birds the range in Argentina, Chile and neighbouring countries is given, expressed in degrees of latitude for direct comparison with the map of southern South America. For pelagic seabirds the breeding distribution is given as well as some indication of the extent of migrations.

The Plumage of a Bird

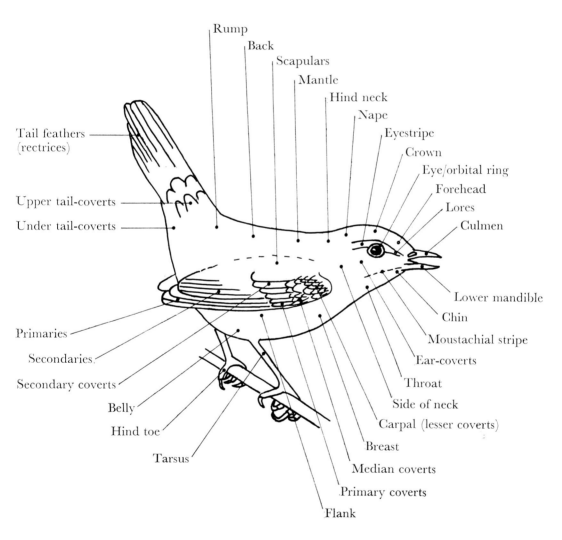

Rump
Back
Scapulars
Mantle
Hind neck
Nape
Eyestripe
Crown
Eye/orbital ring
Forehead
Lores
Culmen

Tail feathers
(rectrices)

Upper tail-coverts

Under tail-coverts

Lower mandible

Chin

Moustachial stripe

Ear-coverts

Throat

Side of neck

Carpal (lesser coverts)

Breast

Median coverts

Primary coverts

Flank

Primaries

Secondaries

Secondary coverts

Belly

Hind toe

Tarsus

FIG. 4.

FIELD GUIDE

ABOVE LEFT Adult Gentoo Penguin, chick & egg at nest on
Port Harriet Pt., East Falkland (*see p.* 68).
ABOVE RIGHT Adult Magellanic Penguin, Yorke Bay, East Falkland (*see p.* 73).
BELOW Landing Bay, Kidney I.

King Penguin

Aptenodytes patagonicus Miller   A. & C. Pingüino rey

IDENTIFICATION. Gigantic. 36–38″. This handsome bird is *larger than any other Falkland penguin* and can only be confused with the Emperor, a very rare straggler to these islands. The King is separated from the Emperor by its smaller size, *longer slender bill with a broad orange-red patch* on the lower mandible, and a different colour pattern on head and neck. Head and foreneck are black, with a *large comma-shaped yellow ear-patch*, extending as a narrow band to meet a golden patch on the breast. A narrow black line running from the base of the flipper to the sides of the neck separates blue-grey upperparts from white underparts. Feet black. The immature has paler yellow patches and lacks the red bill patch. The fledgling is covered in a thick, woolly, brown down, looks grotesquely fat and is quite unmistakable. Noticeably more tame and less disturbed by human intrusion than other penguins, it is usually seen singly and with Gentoo or Magellanic Penguins.

VOICE. The adults' usual call is a musical trumpeting uttered with the bill pointing skywards. This call is loud and easily recognized. The call of a first year bird is a clear, soft, triple whistle.

FOOD. Mainly cuttlefish and small fish.

HABITAT, STATUS & BREEDING. Prefers flat ground near the shore when breeding. More than a century ago it was a numerous breeding species, but as happened in other parts of its range, it was virtually exterminated by sealers and collectors of penguin-oil by 1870. Since then only occasional birds were recorded until about thirty years ago, when one or two very small colonies were found near Cow Bay. In recent years up to about twenty pairs have been known to breed near Gentoo colonies at Volunteer Point, on East Falkland. Only one pale olive-green egg is laid, probably in November or December. It

ABOVE White-tufted Grebe near its nest on Bertha's Beach Pond, East Falkland (*see p.* 74). BELOW Bertha's Beach Pond.

67

makes no nest; the egg is incubated on the feet and covered by the tail and a loose fold of skin in front. The egg is covered so completely that a casual observer would not know that the bird was incubating.

DISTRIBUTION ABROAD. Circumpolar; on sub-antarctic and low antarctic islands. In the South Atlantic it was formerly abundant at the South Shetlands and in Tierra del Fuego, but it is rare at these islands now, although it still breeds at Staten I. and Horn I. Still apparently numerous at islands of the South Sandwich group and increasing at South Georgia. It is a sedentary species that remains near its breeding grounds throughout the year.

Gentoo Penguin

Pygoscelis papua (Forster)   A. Pingüino pico rojo   C. Not recorded

IDENTIFICATION. Very large. c30″. The largest common Falkland penguin, easily recognized by a *white bar over the crown* and the *long bright orange bill with black culmen*. Head black; frequently with a scattering of white feathers other than the crown bar. Plumage blue-black above becoming brown when worn. White underparts. Legs and feet orange. Immature resembles adult, apart from a slighter bill and shorter tail. Very inquisitive and will approach close to an observer if he remains still, but also panics and rushes away if suddenly disturbed. Walks in a leisurely manner by traditional and often circuitous routes to colonies which are frequently up to a mile inland. (Colour photo: p. 65)

VOICE. Has a variety of calls, the most frequent being a loud trumpeting uttered with the head thrown up. A higher pitched 'wha-r-r-r' is heard in courtship or when disturbed on the nest. A short 'caw' is often used when coming ashore, or at sea when resting at the surface. Young in the nest have a quavering squeak and a quiet, peeping note.

FOOD. The main diet consists of crustaceans, cuttlefish and fish.

HABITAT, STATUS & BREEDING. This is the only penguin to be seen ashore in numbers throughout the winter in the Falkland Is. Very numerous and widely spread, it nests on outlying islands and many parts of the East and West mainland. Colonies, which vary from thirty to thousands of pairs, use comparatively flat ground, often amongst diddle-dee. This plant is torn up and used as nest material and is also killed by the penguins' droppings, which fertilize the ground and cause the grass to grow well the following year. These facts, coupled with their habit of changing the site of a colony each year, have earned the Gentoo a good reputation in the eyes of the sheep-farmers. The nest is a substantial structure of grass and twigs in which usually 2 spherical white eggs are laid between late September and mid-October. If the eggs are collected for human consumption or otherwise lost, replacement clutches are laid, but in second or subsequent layings the eggs are smaller.

DISTRIBUTION ABROAD. Circumpolar in the west wind zone of the Antarctic, breeding at all low antarctic islands except Bouvet. It also reaches at least 65°S in the Antarctic Peninsula and breeds at Staten I. At South Georgia, Kerguelen, Macquarie and the Falklands it is apparently resident, but those breeding at more southerly colonies migrate to sea during winter. Although the extent of their migrations is unknown, some winter north to about 43°S on the coast of Argentina.

Rockhopper Penguin

Eudyptes crestatus (Miller)   A. & C. Pingüino de penacho amarillo
Local name: Rocky

IDENTIFICATION. Large. c25″. The *smallest* penguin breeding in the Falklands, it is recognized by a *bright yellow eyebrow* culminating in *long yellow plumes* behind the small red eye. Throat and head black with a spiky frill on the crown, which is raised when excited. Upper surface blue-black in new plumage becoming brown when worn. Underparts white. Bill stout, very strong; colour varies between orange and red. The male has a longer, stouter bill than the female, otherwise the sexes are alike. Legs and feet pink. Immature resembles adults but is duller with pale yellow eyebrow and lacks plumes. A very noisy and quarrelsome bird, adept at climbing very steep rock faces in a series of bounds with both feet together.

VOICE. The noise from a large colony is quite deafening at close quarters, and may be heard at any time of day or night. The call is a short, loud bark, harsh and grating, repeated rhythmically. Cobb likened it to the sound of a rusty wheelbarrow being pushed at full speed. The chick has a single, plaintive 'peeeep' call.

FOOD. Mainly crustaceans; also takes fish.

HABITAT, STATUS & BREEDING. Very numerous around the coasts and islands of the Falklands. Returns from its winter pelagic wanderings in late September and October to breed in closely-packed colonies on cliff-tops and steep cliff-sides. Colonies are often found in association with those of King Cormorant and Black-browed Albatross. 2 pear-shaped, whitish, limy eggs

69

Rockhopper Penguins nesting on Kidney Island.

are laid during the last days of October and early November in a shallow hollow of tussock stems, or simply a depression in peaty soil. Where the path to a colony crosses a stream, especially in thick tussock, the ground becomes very boggy and on warm days the odour is extremely pungent. Adults and young, having moulted, leave the breeding-sites and by mid-April the colonies are almost deserted.

DISTRIBUTION ABROAD. Circumpolar in the sub-antarctic zone. It breeds at islands of Tierra del Fuego, Tristan da Cunha, Gough, Prince Edward, Crozet, Kerguelen, St. Paul and Amsterdam in the South Atlantic and southern Indian Ocean, and at Macquarie, Campbell and other islands in the South Pacific. Ranges north in winter to about 35°S, but little is known about movements.

Macaroni Penguin

Eudyptes chrysolophus (Brandt)   A. Pingüino anaranjado   C. Not recorded

IDENTIFICATION. Large. 27–28″. Resembles the Rockhopper in habits and colour, but it has *golden-yellow head plumes springing from a patch of the same colour on the forehead*, drooping back and out over its eyes. Also, the Macaroni's dark throat area finishes in a 'V' while the demarcation line on the Rockhopper is almost straight across the throat. The bill is larger and heavier than the Rockhopper's; brownish-black with a red tip and *a small patch of pink skin showing at the base*; the iris is dull red. Sexes are alike, although the male is slightly larger. The immature resembles the adult but it has fewer and paler yellow head plumes.

VOICE. The usual call is a loud trumpeting, harsher and deeper than that of the Gentoo.

FOOD. Crustaceans and cuttlefish.

HABITAT, STATUS & BREEDING. Rare in the Falkland Is. and breeding in very small numbers in association with Rockhoppers. 2 white eggs are laid though only the second larger egg is incubated. It seems to lay later than the Rockhopper, probably in mid-November. No data on arrivals and departures from the Falklands are available, but they are almost certainly similar to those of the Rockhopper. Single birds have been recorded from various places in the Islands, but the majority of breeding records have come from the northeast of East Falkland.

DISTRIBUTION ABROAD. The Macaroni is a bird of the colder sub-antarctic

islands, and breeds at South Georgia, South Shetlands, South Orkneys and South Sandwich islands in the South Atlantic, and at islands in the southern Indian Ocean. Little is known of its habits outside the breeding-season, and it is not known if long pelagic migrations are made.

Magellanic Penguin

Spheniscus magellanicus (Forster)
A. Pingüino de Magallanes   C. Pingüino del sur
Local name: Jackass

IDENTIFICATION. Large to very large. c28″. This species is decidedly more shy than other Falkland penguins, and is easily recognized by the *conspicuous pattern of black and white bands crossing the throat and neck and extending down to the flanks*. The head is black with a broad white band from either side of the crown, looping behind the cheeks and meeting on the throat. Upper surface dark slate-grey; underparts white, often with a few scattered black feathers. Lores sparsely feathered showing a variable amount of pink skin. Bill rather short, but very stout and strong. Both bill and feet are blackish, barred and flecked with white. An immature bird, up to one year old has greyish throat and fore-neck and lacks the striking head pattern. Although so shy that it rapidly retreats to its burrow or the sea when disturbed, in the nest burrow it vigorously defends itself with its extremely sharp, strong bill. (Colour photo: p. 65)

VOICE. The local name of Jackass is derived from its loud braying call, frequently uttered at the entrance to the burrow, and also heard from birds afloat offshore. The call is composed of four or five short honks alternating with sudden intakes of breath and reaching a crescendo with a long-drawn howl that rises and then falls in pitch as it dies away. Well-grown young in the nest burrow give a monotonous repeated 'pee-pee-pee-pee'.

FOOD. Cuttlefish and small sprat-like fish.

HABITAT, STATUS & BREEDING. A numerous summer resident, returning in early September and leaving about mid-April, although occasional birds are seen during the winter. Breeds in large and small colonies around both main islands and on most of the outlying islands. Colonies are near the shore. Nest burrows are dug in peat and sandy soil, usually between 4 and 6 ft. deep. The nest is a pile of diddle-dee or tussock-grass. The tunnel always slopes down, but the nest-chamber floor is slightly higher than the adjacent tunnel floor, so that water which often runs into the burrows tends to collect away from the

Immature Macaroni Penguin.

eggs. 2 white eggs are laid between mid-October and mid-November, but they soon become badly stained.

DISTRIBUTION ABROAD. Breeds in southern South America from 41°S in Argentina and 37°S in Chile to Tierra del Fuego; also at Juan Fernandez (34°S) off the coast of Chile. Most numerous in the Magellanic region. Ranges north on migration to 30°S in Chile and to southern Brazil, occasionally reaching Rio de Janeiro (23°S).

White-tufted Grebe

Podiceps rolland rolland (Quoy et Gaimard)
A. Macá común   C. Zambullidor pimpollo
Local names: Brown, Black or Golden Grebe, Hell Diver

IDENTIFICATION. Small-medium. c14″. A round-bodied, almost tail-less water-bird. *Peaked head, slender neck and upperparts are black* with a metallic green sheen, save for a *triangular patch of white plumes* streaked with black *on the cheeks* (summer only). The underparts are rich chestnut, streaked with black on the flanks. The very short black tail has white under tail-coverts. Iris glowing crimson; sharp-pointed bill black. In winter it has a white throat, dull red-brown foreneck and whitish underparts. The immature resembles a winter adult but has two blackish lines across the white cheeks. At a distance it can be confused with the Rock Cormorant, but *the latter has a longer head and bill, usually uptilted.* It is tame and inquisitive. Pairs tend to remain together throughout the year. On the infrequent occasions when it flies, shows a broad whitish wing-bar. (Colour photo: p. 66)

VOICE. The call is a quiet creaking note, higher-pitched in the young, but it is usually silent outside the breeding-season.

FOOD. Takes fish up to about 6 in. long, crustaceans and aquatic plants. All food is obtained underwater by diving, using only its lobed feet for propulsion. The average dive lasts about 15 seconds, and the maximum recorded is about 20 seconds.

HABITAT, STATUS & BREEDING. Mainly found on freshwater ponds, streams and rivers; in winter also on creeks and the sea close to the shore. Fairly common throughout the Islands. Breeds between mid-October and January, laying 1–3 eggs, which are white at first, but rapidly become stained. The floating nest, built of water-weeds and grass, is placed under the over-hanging edge of a pond or stream, or among rushes. Nests in streams are sometimes washed away by sudden floods. Nests are often difficult to locate as the eggs are covered by nest materials when the bird leaves.

DISTRIBUTION ABROAD. The race *Podiceps r. rolland* is confined to the Falkland Is. A smaller race, *P. r. chilensis*, inhabits South America except the Andes from 10°S in Peru through Bolivia, Paraguay, southeast Brazil, Uruguay, Chile and most of Argentina to Tierra del Fuego.

Silvery Grebe

Podiceps occipitalis (Garnot)
A. Macá plateado   C. Zambullidor blanquillo común
Local name: White Grebe

IDENTIFICATION. Small. c11″. Slightly smaller than the White-tufted Grebe from which it is easily distinguished by its *shining white foreneck, jet-black nape and hind neck*. Back and wing-coverts are dark grey-brown; crown, sides of head and throat light grey. Underparts white, but flanks are streaked with black. The adult in summer has *a large frill of dull gold facial plumes* extending from eyebrow to ear-coverts, but these are completely lacking in winter. Iris bright crimson; sharp-pointed bill, legs and feet black. The immature is similar to the adult in winter, but the hind neck is white tinged with brown, not black. It dives frequently and is reluctant to fly, but when it does, shows a white wing-bar. Small chicks are carried and sheltered on the back of one parent, while the other parent dives and collects food which is passed to the chick.

VOICE. No information on call-notes is available.

FOOD. Obtains all its food, which consists of aquatic plants, small crustaceans, fish and fish eggs, by diving.

HABITAT, STATUS & BREEDING. Widely distributed throughout the Islands and in the breeding-season often found on the same freshwater ponds as the White-tufted Grebe, although it is not as common. There are several records of small parties being seen amongst coastal kelp patches, in the autumn, which suggests at least a local migration. Very little information is available on its breeding in the Falkland Is. It lays 2 blue-white eggs, which soon become stained by the weeds that form the floating nest. The breeding-season is uncertain, but it probably lays during the period October to December.

DISTRIBUTION ABROAD. *P. o. occipitalis* is also found in Chile and Argentina from Tierra del Fuego north to about 25°S. It is replaced in the Andean regions of northern Chile and northern Argentina, north to Peru, Ecuador and Colombia by another race, *P. o. juninensis*.

Wandering Albatross

Diomedea exulans Linn.   A. & C. Albatros errante

Royal Albatross

Diomedea epomophora Lesson   A. & C. Albatros real
Local name: Albatross

IDENTIFICATION. Gigantic. Wandering, 44–53″; Royal, 41–45″. Wingspan c10′. Both of these species are *much larger* than the common Black-browed Albatross and can be recognized by size alone, but the adult and immature Royal and adult male 'Wanderer' all have *mainly white plumage with black wing-tips*, so they cannot be separately distinguished at sea. Some adult female 'Wanderers' have a brown cap and variable brown vermiculations on the back and flanks. The juvenile 'Wanderer' is brown apart from white forehead, lores, throat and under wing-coverts. The brown plumage is gradually replaced by white with increasing age, so young birds are variably mottled brown and white, but always show a white underwing.

HABITAT, STATUS & RECORDS. Albatrosses of either or both these species are often seen in Falkland waters, particularly in winter and off the west side of the Islands. Cawkell (C. & H. 1961) stated that the Wandering Albatross was found breeding in small numbers at Beauchêne I. (52°54′S 59°11′W) nearly 40 miles south of the main East Falkland group in January 1959. G. Reid of the Directorate of Overseas Surveys who visited the island on 6th January 1959, reported 'a fair number of larger albatrosses nesting among the Black-browed Albatrosses' (personal communication). A. G. Denton-Thompson, then Colonial Secretary in Stanley, also visited the island on 21st December 1959 and reported one large immature albatross flapping through the small Gentoo Penguin colony (personal communication). However, survey parties from H.M.S. *Protector* visiting Beauchêne I. in December 1962, 1963 and 1964 reported seeing only Black-browed Albatrosses (Strange, 1965).

DISTRIBUTION ABROAD. *Wandering Albatross:* breeds at the antarctic and sub-antarctic islands of South Georgia, Prince Edward, Crozet, Kerguelen, Campbell, Auckland and Antipodes. A smaller race breeds at Tristan da Cunha and Gough I. The flight range is circumpolar in the westerly wind belt between the Tropic of Capricorn and 60°S. *Royal Albatross:* known from the South Atlantic and South Pacific, it breeds at Campbell, Auckland and Chatham Is. near New Zealand, and at Taiaroa Head, South I., New Zealand. Dabbene believed, from information supplied by Reynolds, that this species bred in the interior of Tierra del Fuego (Murphy, 1936), but no recent records have confirmed this theory and it now seems most unlikely to breed in the South American region. The flight-range extends north to the Kermadec Is., central Chile (where New Zealand banded birds have been recovered), and Peru. Campbell I. birds have been found in the western South Atlantic, north to the Uruguayan coast, and it has reached 23°S on the coast of Brazil.

Black-browed Albatross

Diomedea melanophris Temminck
A. Albatros chico   C. Albatros de ceja negra
Local name: Mollymawk

IDENTIFICATION. Very large to immense. 28–33″. Wingspan 8′. A *very large* seabird, *blackish above* on wings and tail, with *pure white head, neck, rump and underparts*. It is recognized by its *large hooked, pink-yellow bill* and a black line over and through the eye, giving it a scowling expression. The underside of the wings is mainly white, but broadly edged with blackish in front and narrowly edged behind. In flight shows very long narrow wings and has the gliding circling action typical of all Albatrosses. The juvenile has a black bill, a variable grey patch on the nape and sides of the neck, and the underside of the wing mainly dark with a white line down the centre. In intermediate plumage immature birds have a white head and a dull, brownish bill. An immature bird is not easily distinguished at sea from the immature Yellow-nosed and Grey-headed Albatrosses. (Colour photos: pp. 83, 84)

VOICE. The adult has a loud braying note used frequently during courtship and at the nest. At sea it is usually silent, but a croaking note is sometimes used when feeding.

FOOD. Chiefly squids, lobster-krill and small fish. It also takes refuse from ships at sea. Occasionally forces petrels to disgorge and attacks wounded or dead birds.

HABITAT, STATUS & BREEDING. Common in Falkland waters between September and April. Pelagic outside the breeding-season, although small numbers are seen during the winter. Breeds in colonies, often numbering tens of thousands, on the steep slopes of a number of islands off West Falkland, the largest being at Bird I. Another very large colony exists at Beauchêne I., 40 miles south of East Falkland. There is only one very small colony on the northwest point of West Falkland. Rookeries of Rockhopper Penguins frequently adjoin or are intermingled with the albatross colonies. Nests are solid structures of mud and grass in the form of pillars with a depression on top. The single large white egg, with variable red-brown markings mainly around the large end, is laid in October, and the fledged young leave the nest from mid-March to early April.

DISTRIBUTION ABROAD. Breeds at islets near Cape Horn, Staten I., South Georgia, Kerguelen, Heard, Prince Edward, Campbell and Auckland Is. Ranges northward in the Pacific, Indian and South Atlantic Oceans to about 13°S, and southward to about 60°S.

Since 1960 nearly eleven thousand nestlings have been banded at West Point I., Falkland Is.; three thousand each in 1962 and 1963; nearly two thousand each in 1964 and 1965 and the remainder in 1960 and 1961. Recoveries of some of these young birds after leaving the nest have been made by Argentinian and Brazilian fishermen who catch them at sea. Others have been found dead or dying on the coasts of Buenos Aires province in Argentina, Uruguay and south-east Brazil north to Cape Frio (23°S). Four birds banded in 1962 were caught at sea or found dead on the coasts of the Republic of South Africa between two and a half and six months after leaving the Falkland Is. One bird reached 16°S on the coast of Angola in mid-July 1963, about three and a half months after leaving West Point I. These recoveries seem to show that young Black-browed Albatrosses from the Falkland Is. travel north along the east coast of South America, where many are seen in winter, while some cross the South Atlantic to South African waters when others are still off the Argentine coast. These are mostly recoveries made in the bird's first year of life, but it appears probable that a small proportion of immature birds complete a circular migration in the South Atlantic, while the majority travel north and south off the Argentina-Uruguay-southeast Brazil coasts before returning to the Falkland Is. in their fourth or fifth year.

Grey-headed Albatross

Diomedea chrysostoma Forster   A. & C. Albatros cabeza gris

IDENTIFICATION. Very large. 28–32″. Similar to the Black-browed Albatross in size, habits and general colouration, the adult is recognized by its *slate-grey head and blackish bill with a yellow stripe down the centre of the upper mandible* and yellow at the base of the lower mandible. As the extent of the grey on the head is variable, separation from the Yellow-nosed Albatross is often difficult. (The Yellow-nosed has an all-white head.) On a closer view, the adult shows a black stripe through the eye and a white lower eyelid. Juvenile and immature birds cannot be reliably separated at sea from those of the Black-browed. The juvenile usually has a mainly grey-brown head, but some are little darker on the head than the darkest juvenile Black-browed.

HABITAT, STATUS & RECORDS. Infrequently recorded in Falkland seas and not known to breed in the Falkland Is., although adults have been recorded amongst Black-browed Albatrosses at West Point I. One adult occupying a nest at West Point was banded in October 1952, and returned each year till 1956, but has not been seen since. It was apparently unmated as it was always seen alone.

DISTRIBUTION ABROAD. The flight range is circumpolar in the westerly wind belt between the northern limit of pack-ice and about 40°S. This species, which is apparently less numerous than the Black-browed, breeds at many of the islands occupied by the Black-browed, e.g. Diego Ramirez and Ildefonso off Cape Horn, South Georgia, Prince Edward, Kerguelen and Campbell Is., but as it seems to prefer islands with a colder climate, it is absent from the more temperate islands in the Black-browed Albatross' range, e.g. Falkland, Antipodes and Auckland Is.

Sooty Albatross

Phoebetria fusca (Hilsenberg)   A. & C. Albatros oscuro

Light-mantled Sooty Albatross

Phoebetria palpebrata (Forster)
A. Albatros oscuro   C. Albatros oscuro de manto claro

IDENTIFICATION. Very large. c30″. Both species are *more slender* than other albatrosses and have *very graceful flight*. The *wings are all dark* above and below and the *tail is long and wedge-shaped*.

Sooty Albatross: mainly dark sooty-brown, darker on the head and wings. *Bill black with a bright yellow line on the lower mandible.* The immature has a whitish collar.

Light-mantled Sooty Albatross: head and wings dark greyish-brown; *the back is pale ashy-grey* and the underparts darker. *Bill black with an indistinct bluish line* on the lower mandible. The immature is indistinguishable from the adult.

HABITAT, STATUS & RECORDS. 'Sooty Albatrosses' have been noted occasionally in Falkland seas, but there are few records with specific identification. The Light-mantled Sooty is apparently more frequent, but an individual of the northern species, *P. fusca*, was photographed in December 1953 by Pettingill on Kidney I., East Falkland, where it spent three days on an old King Cormorant nest (E. R. Pettingill, 1962). A single 'Sooty Albatross' was seen briefly near Kidney I. on 1st November 1962.

DISTRIBUTION ABROAD. *P. fusca* is found only in the temperate South Atlantic and Indian Oceans from about 30°S to 55°S, and breeds at Tristan da Cunha, Gough, St. Paul and Amsterdam Is. *P. palpebrata* is of circumpolar distribution in sub-antarctic and antarctic regions, ranging north to about 20°S off the Chilean coast and south to beyond the antarctic circle (66½°S). It breeds at most cold sub-antarctic islands, the nearest station to the Falkland Is. being South Georgia.

Giant Petrel

Macronectes giganteus (Gmelin)   A. & C. Petrel gigante
Local name: Stinker

IDENTIFICATION. Immense. 33–36″. Wingspan 7′. *Much larger than any other petrel* and about the same size as the Black-browed Albatross. The adult is recognized by its *predominantly grey-brown plumage and a whitish head*. The *juvenile is completely slaty-black at first* and fades to very dark brown with increasing age. *A white phase, only marked with a few dark flecks*, and in which the immature is indistinguishable from the adult, is found more commonly in the colder parts of its range. Its flight silhouette is distinctive; the long narrow angled wings appear to be set too far back, about midway between the short rounded tail and the large head with its *very heavy pale cream or greenish bill*. It is not a graceful flyer and looks ungainly as it flaps frequently in light winds. In a gale it is more agile and can glide with ease and speed for long distances. It is a familiar bird in Stanley harbour, where it consorts with Kelp Gulls scavenging offal and waste matter, particularly at the slaughterhouse outflow pipe. (Colour photo: p. 101)

VOICE. Like other petrels, it is usually silent at sea, but when scrambling for offal frequently uses a low guttural rattling note, 'arrrrrr'. During courtship it utters a mewing note, and when flying over the breeding ground has a long drawn neighing call.

FOOD. It is well known as a scavenger and killer. It takes all kinds of carrion, e.g. from dead seals and penguins and whale carcasses; also takes ships' refuse, squids and crustaceans at sea. It kills young penguins, takes eggs, kills any weak or disabled seabirds it finds and is known to attack cast sheep.

HABITAT, STATUS & BREEDING. This large, conspicuous species was not mentioned by Darwin in 1833/34, perhaps because it was much less common than it is now. However, it is probable that the growth of sheep-farming in the latter half of the 19th century and early 20th century enabled it to increase its numbers. Since then the breeding population seems to have declined due to shooting and egg-taking by man because it is considered a menace to the sheep. It is now commonly found all round the Falkland Is. throughout the year, and is the only petrel that habitually enters Stanley harbour. The main colonies are on Elephant Cays, Steeple Jason and Sea Lion I., each with one hundred or more pairs. It has been recorded near a colony in mid-August, but it lays its single large white egg in late October. On George I., where there was a small colony of about thirty pairs in November 1961, the nests were mere scrapes in 'black ground' (bare, decomposed peat, previously covered by tussock-grass, but eaten out by sheep and eroded by wind and rain). On Sea Lion I. the egg is laid in a hollow in the sand.

DISTRIBUTION ABROAD. Circumpolar from Antarctica to about 23°S, but almost reaching the Equator in the Humboldt Current and off the west coast of Africa. It breeds at sub-antarctic and antarctic islands including South Georgia, South Orkneys, Gough and South Shetlands, and at islands south of New Zealand and Australia, as well as on the antarctic continent. Young birds, when newly fledged, perform tremendous flights, sometimes covering 10,000 miles in six weeks. This has been shown by recoveries of banded birds from Signy I., South Orkneys, which indicate that they disperse northwards as far as $12\frac{1}{2}$°S off Africa and eastwards to Australia and New Zealand, where many exhausted birds are driven ashore by strong winds.

Silver-grey Fulmar

Fulmarus glacialoides Stephens   A. & C. Petrel plateado

IDENTIFICATION. Medium. 18–20″. Wingspan 4′. A fairly large petrel with long narrow wings and short rounded tail, it is *pale grey above* with a white forehead and *white underparts*. The *wing-tips are black with a variable* but usually discernible *whitish patch*. The rather heavy, hooked bill is mainly pink. It has the typical stiff-winged gliding flight of Fulmars.

HABITAT, STATUS & RECORDS. Frequently recorded in Falkland seas during most of the year, but more numerous in winter and early summer. In December 1954 and late November 1958 a dozen or more were seen in Port William, the outer Stanley harbour.

DISTRIBUTION ABROAD. Circumpolar in the Antarctic, it breeds on the continent and at a number of islands, including the South Orkneys and Kerguelen. On migration northward it is numerous throughout the sub-antarctic regions, ranges almost to the Equator in the South Atlantic and sometimes crosses into the North Pacific from the Humboldt Current zone.

Cape Petrel

Daption capense (Linn.)
A. Petrel común, Damero del cabo   C. Petrel moteado

IDENTIFICATION. Small-medium. 14–16″. Wingspan 3′. One of the easiest petrels to recognize; *its back and wings are heavily chequered black and white*. The head and tail are black and all the underparts are white. The bill is blackish.

HABITAT, STATUS & RECORDS. A common winter visitor and passage-migrant, most numerous around the Falkland Is. between late April and November, when it is often seen close inshore.

DISTRIBUTION ABROAD. Circumpolar in antarctic and cold sub-antarctic regions, it breeds on the antarctic continent and at many islands. Ranges north on migration commonly to the Equator in the Humboldt Current and occasionally reaches 40–50°N in the Atlantic and Pacific Oceans.

Blue Petrel

Halobaena caerulea (Gmelin)   A. & C. Petrel azulado

IDENTIFICATION. Small. 11–12″. Closely resembles the Slender-billed Prion, with which it associates at sea, but is recognized by its *square, white-tipped tail*, black, hook-tipped bill, slightly larger size, and black mottling on the white forehead. The Blue Petrel and all Prions are blue-grey above with *dark markings on wings and back forming an inverted 'W' pattern* in flight.

HABITAT, STATUS & RECORDS. There is much confusion between the Blue Petrel and the Slender-billed Prion, and the former was thought to breed in the Falkland Is., but no breeding specimens have been found. It is occasionally recorded in Falkland seas, but is much more numerous near South Georgia, south of the Falkland Is. towards the Antarctic Peninsula, and in the Cape Horn area.

Two nestling Black-browed Albatrosses perched precariously on Devil's
Nose rookery, West Point (*see p.* 77); Rockhopper Penguins are
ascending the lower slopes of Cliff Mt. behind.

DISTRIBUTION ABROAD. Widespread in the west-wind zone of the southern oceans, it ranges north in the Humboldt Current as far as 33°S and south to the edge of pack-ice. It is only known to breed at Heard, Crozet, Kerguelen and Macquarie Is., but it may breed at Staten I. off Tierra del Fuego.

Slender-billed Prion

Pachyptila belcheri (Mathews)   A. Petrel ballena pico delgado
C. Petrel-paloma de pico delgado   Local name: Firebird

IDENTIFICATION. Small. c11″. A small petrel, *blue-grey above* with a dark inverted 'W' mark across the wings, *black-tipped tail*, *white underparts* and a broad white line over and behind the eye. The bill and feet are blue. It is considerably larger than the Grey-backed Storm-Petrel and has very rapid twisting flight. Prions are often seen in large flocks which seem to appear and disappear as they twist and turn, showing first their white underparts and then their blue-grey backs. Two other species of prion, the Broad-billed (*P. forsteri*) and Dove (*P desolata*) have been recorded at the Falkland Is. as vagrants, but it is almost impossible to distinguish between species of prion in flight. Refer to Murphy (1936) for specific features of prions in the hand.

VOICE. In the nest burrow a guttural cooing note is used, and a peeping note has also been recorded. E. M. Cawkell noted that at a large colony, thousands of them calling at night sounded like the heavy roar of surf.

FOOD. No definite records are available, but it probably feeds mainly on crustaceans and small fish found near the sea surface.

HABITAT, STATUS & BREEDING. This species is probably one of the commoner breeding petrels in the Falkland Is.; it returns from migration in August or September to breed, and leaves in March and April. It breeds in very large colonies at New I., Grand Jason and Steeple Jason and in smaller numbers at other islands. Only one colony on East Falkland is known, at Macbride Head. The nest burrows are usually close together; they vary from 2 to 5 ft. in depth and are excavated in slopes of peat or sand beneath tussock-grass and turf, also in the sides of eroded peat banks and under rocks. The single white egg is probably laid in October or November.

DISTRIBUTION ABROAD. The Slender-billed Prion is a little-known species that breeds at Kerguelen and almost certainly breeds on Staten I. and in other parts of Tierra del Fuego. It migrates north at least as far as 24°S in the South Atlantic and has reached 15°S on the Pacific coast of Chile. It is also regularly recorded in Australasian seas.

Adult Black-browed Albatross on empty nest, West Point I. (*see p.* 77).   85

Fairy Prion

Pachyptila turtur Kuhl   A. Petrel ballena chico   C. Not recorded

IDENTIFICATION. Small. c10″. Somewhat smaller than *P. belcheri* and probably indistinguishable in flight, though it is said to be bluer and the black tail tip covers the whole terminal half of the tail. The bill is slightly shorter and broader than that of *P. belcheri*. Murphy (1936) gives the following dimensions from ten specimens of each species:

	Greatest Bill Width	Exposed Culmen
P. belcheri	10·6 (9·8–11·4)mm	25·9 (23·7–28·3)mm
P. turtur	10·9 (10–11·8)mm	23·3 (21·8–24·2)mm

VOICE. Strange (1968) noted that both adults and young called at night at the breeding ground on Beauchêne I.

FOOD. Murphy notes that small crustaceans have been found in specimens from Bounty I.

HABITAT, STATUS & BREEDING. Found breeding for the first time in the Falkland Is. in January 1967 (Strange, 1968). A small colony was discovered nesting about 3 ft. beneath rock slabs on the southern end of Beauchêne I. Chicks in down were found and many broken eggshells were seen at the surface. There is only one previous record, a bird found newly dead near Stanley on 11th March 1917 (Bennett, 1926).

DISTRIBUTION ABROAD. Breeds on sub-antarctic islands near New Zealand and ranges in the Pacific and Indian Oceans to about 35°S; it has only rarely been recorded from the South Atlantic.

Shoemaker

Procellaria aequinoctialis Linn.
A. Petrel negro   C. Fardela negra grande
Local names: Cobbler, Night Hawk

IDENTIFICATION. Medium-large. 20–21″. Wingspan 5′. A *large black petrel* with a *very pale greenish bill*, the plumage above and below is sooty-black, sometimes appearing dark brown in strong sunlight. Most individuals have a white chin, but this is very variable in extent and not often seen in flight. It is separated from the Sooty Shearwater by larger size, *dark undersides of broader wings* and pale

Shoemaker near its burrow.

bill. It can be confused with the juvenile Giant Petrel, but is much smaller, has a shorter neck and lacks the Giant Petrel's massive bill. It gathers with Sooty Shearwaters milling over the breeding ground at dusk when it can be separated by its more leisurely flight; the wing-beats are slower and it often glides quite long distances. Although it is mainly nocturnal at the breeding ground, some return and land in broad daylight.

VOICE. Outside the breeding-season it is a silent bird. In flight over its burrows and when on the ground it utters a very loud, shrill, screaming trill, 'chiky-chiky-chiky-chiky . . .'. A low quiet 'unk-unk' has been heard from a bird at its burrow entrance.

FOOD. Squids are the main diet; it also takes crustaceans and fish.

HABITAT, STATUS & BREEDING. This species is a summer resident in the Falkland Is.; adults probably arrive in early October and leave by the end of March, but there is little information on arrival and departure. It is not known when the fledged young leave their burrows. It is only known to breed on Kidney I., off the east coast of East Falkland, where the nest burrows of a few hundred pairs are concentrated mainly along the south-facing slope in a band about 15 yd. wide from the beach. Burrows in the soft tussock-peat are often over 6 ft. long and usually curved. They are renovated or excavated in October. The nest is a slightly raised platform of peat and dry grass upon which the single large white egg is laid in late October or November.

TABLE 2. *Shoemakers Banded and Recaught at Kidney I.*

Banded		Recaught		
Year	Number	1961	1962	1963
1960	5	1	3	1
1961	44	1	10	2
1962	22		1	1

Seventy-one adults, all caught by hand at or near their burrows, were banded on Kidney I. between December 1960 and October 1962, as shown in the Table. This also shows the numbers of individuals recaught later in the same or following seasons. Only two birds were recaught in two consecutive years following the year of banding.

DISTRIBUTION ABROAD. *P. aequinoctialis* breeds in large numbers at South Georgia, and also at the Crozets, Kerguelen and sub-antarctic islands near New Zealand. Its flight range in winter extends north to about 6°S off Peru and 30°S off Brazil, occasionally reaching the Equator.

Greater Shearwater

Puffinus gravis (O'Reilly)   A. Petrel pardo   C. Not recorded

IDENTIFICATION. Medium. c18″. A large Shearwater, mainly dark brown above and white beneath, recognized by its *dark brown cap contrasting with white cheeks, and a narrow white half-moon at the base of the tail.* The white on the face extends round the neck so that it almost separates the dark cap from the brown mantle. The underside of the wing is mainly white, but marked with brown at the leading edge and on the axillaries. It has an indistinct brown patch on the belly. The slender bill is very dark brown and has a sharply hooked tip.

VOICE. When squabbling over food at sea it uses various harsh notes. During courtship and the breeding-season it utters a loud shieking call, described by M. K. Rowan (1952) as 'ma-ma-ma-ma-ma-ma . . .' or 'ha-ha-ha-ha-ha-ha . . .' with longer notes at the start rising in pitch and quickening to a climax.

FOOD. Chiefly squids, which are caught on the surface and by 'flying' underwater; it also takes fish and discharged refuse from boats.

HABITAT, STATUS & BREEDING. Until 1954 it was only known as a visitor to Falkland seas, recorded in summer and winter. In February 1954, Dr. and Mrs. Pettingill saw several coming into Kidney I. at night. On 28th December 1961, one adult was caught in a burrow on Kidney I. and the following day its mate and a chipped egg were found in the same burrow. A few other burrows in the vicinity appeared similar in shape and one or two contained white breast feathers when examined in mid-January 1962. These burrows were found on the western point of Kidney I. where the greatest concentration of Sooty Shearwaters nest. While watching the evening gatherings of Sooty Shearwaters and Shoemakers over Kidney I., 'white-bellied' (probably Greater) Shearwaters were seen only twice. It is unlikely that many Greater Shearwaters breed but probable that a very small colony has existed on Kidney I. for several years. With an incubation period similar to that found by Rowan for this species on Nightingale I. (seven to eight weeks), the egg found chipped on Kidney I. would have been laid in the second week of November; this coincides with laying dates on Nightingale I. No arrival or departure dates are known for the Falkland Is. (see Woods 1970b).

DISTRIBUTION ABROAD. Until 1961 the only known breeding grounds were at Nightingale, Inaccessible and Gough Is. in the Tristan da Cunha group. It is numerous in both North and South Atlantic from Tierra del Fuego northwards, and during its circular migration, ranges north as far as Labrador, southern Greenland and the Arctic Circle, also reaching the British Isles.

Sooty Shearwater.

Sooty Shearwater

Puffinus griseus (Gmelin)　A. Petrel oscuro común　C. Fardela negra común
Local name: Shyer Bird

IDENTIFICATION. Medium. c16″. Can be separated from the Shoemaker, which is similarly coloured but larger, by its *more slender blackish bill and grey or whitish under wing-coverts*. The plumage is generally dark brown-black above and grey-brown below. Its long narrow wings are noticeable as it flies with rapid shallow wing-beats and stiff-winged glides. In a strong wind it glides long distances, giving an impression of light and then dark plumage as it tilts. When over the breeding-ground after dusk its flight is extremely fast; the wings beat very rapidly and there is little or no gliding (*see* Shoemaker).

VOICE. It rarely calls at sea, but when breeding uses an eerie howling call, 'wheeoo-har', resembling a cat's howling followed by a low sound as the bird takes breath sharply. This call is repeated rhythmically, often sustained unbroken for half a minute, and can be heard from darkness to first light as adults hurtle back and forth above the colony, while others call from their burrows.

of the Jason Is., Gibraltar Rock (by West Point I.) and probably at many more of the outer islands. It is completely nocturnal at its nesting grounds and often overlooked, partly because it does not indulge in mass gatherings in the evenings. Specimens were also found at Triste I. (northeast of Bleaker I.) on 7th May 1962, and at Port Stephens. No information on arrival or departure is available, but it appears to be an early nesting species, returning to the breeding islands in August or September. Nest burrows, which are excavated in soft tussock-peat or in compressed accumulations of dead stems, have entrances about 4 in. wide and $2\frac{1}{2}$ in. high and are at least 3 ft. long. The single rounded white egg is laid in an enlarged chamber probably between late September and late October, but there is little available information. Apparently migrates northward in winter to the coasts of Argentina, reaching at least 38°S.

DISTRIBUTION ABROAD. The race breeding in the Falklands has been described as *P. u. berard*. Several other races occur in a broad sub-antarctic zone in the southern oceans, and breed at Tristan da Cunha, Gough I., Marion I., the Crozets, Kerguelen and Heard Is., at islands southeast of New Zealand and on Tasmanian and adjacent coasts. Another race, not certainly established, has been described from southern Chile, between 47 and 54°S.

Rock Cormorant

Phalacrocorax magellanicus (Gmelin)
A. Viguá cuello negro   C. Cormorán de las rocas
Local name: Black Shag

IDENTIFICATION. Large. c26″. Smaller than the King Cormorant, from which it is separated by its *predominantly black plumage above and on the neck, and the rectangular white area of the underparts*. The black is glossed with purple on head and neck and with green on back and flanks. *The adult has bright orange-red facial skin* and flesh-pink legs and feet. The blackish bill is slender and hooked sharply. The iris colour varies between dark brown and crimson in apparently adult birds. The colouring of head and neck varies considerably; outside the breeding-season most adults have mainly black necks and throats, with variable white flecks, although some show large white patches at midwinter. From mid-October a white auricular patch grows larger and the majority gain white flecking and large white patches on throat and neck, also sometimes a white forehead. Yet even at the height of the breeding-season (December–January) adults are frequently seen with all-black necks. A curved crest grows from the crown from late June onwards; it is lost by early January. On leaving the nest, the juvenile is dark brown with a white belly, but this is soon replaced by brown feathers. *In July a first winter bird is all dark* apart from variable white on the throat. This plumage is retained until the bird is nearly a year old, when white appears again on the belly through wear. Adult plumage is attained soon after the first year of life. The juvenile's legs are black; they gradually become pink after the first year. A rather weak flyer; when taking off almost invariably drops down to the sea surface before gaining any speed. Usually flies low over the water with neck extended and its rounded wings beating very quickly.

VOICE. It is usually silent when alone. Where groups gather to preen after fishing and at the nest, returning birds greet each other with a loud guttural 'karrrk'. In courtship both sexes utter a rapid rhythmic low grunt, 'uk-uk-uk-uk . . .'. Nestlings call a plaintive 'eek' and a continual rasping 'screep' which becomes frantic when parents return with food. (Colour photo: p. 101)

FOOD. Fish, probably small mullet and smelt, which it obtains by diving.

HABITAT, STATUS & BREEDING. A common resident species around the Falkland Is., it is often seen in sheltered harbours and estuaries. It never ventures as far offshore as the King Cormorant, but feeds in shallow water and amongst the kelp patches in sheltered bays. It readily uses jetties, old jetty piles or beached hulks of sailing ships for resting and sometimes nesting. It also occupies the ledges of old hulks used as warehouses which are built onto the ends of jetties at Stanley. Usually nests colonially on ledges of cliffs at least 20 ft. above the sea. The colonies, which vary in size from six to about four hundred nests (398 on Speedwell I. in 1961) are mainly found on cliffs of inlets where they gain some shelter from the wind. Single nests are sometimes seen; one on the top rudder-bearing below the stern of the hulk *Fennia* at anchor in Stanley harbour, was permanently sheltered from all winds as the *Fennia* swung like a giant wind-vane. It sometimes nests on wider flat spaces on cliff tops. Nests are renovated and decorated with small bright pieces of seaweed, dry tussock-grass and sometimes diddle-dee twigs, from the end of September onwards. 2–5, usually 3, greenish-white eggs with chalky deposits are laid between the first days of November and mid-December. Young birds leave the nest between mid-January and the end of February.

DISTRIBUTION ABROAD. Breeds on the coasts of southern South America from 37°S in Chile and 50°S in Argentina to Cape Horn and is particularly common around Tierra del Fuego. Occasionally wanders north as far as 33°S in Chile and to Uruguay (35°S).

King Cormorant

Phalacrocorax albiventer (Lesson)
A. Viguá blanco   C. Cormorán imperial de las Malvinas
Local name: King Shag

IDENTIFICATION. Very large. c29″. The King Cormorant can be separated from the Rock Cormorant, the only other species breeding in the Falkland Is., by *its greater size* and distinctive plumage. It is black above with a metallic blue and green sheen and has *white underparts which extend in an unbroken line to the bill.* A prominent white bar on the inner half of the wing develops in October and is usually lost again by May. A patch of white hair-like plumes above and behind the eye is only present in the early breeding-season, being lost by mid-November. The plumage is brightest between August and October when the orange-yellow caruncles at the culmen base are biggest and a large, untidy, forward-curving black crest on the crown is fully developed. This crest is usually lost during December. The bare facial skin is blue, the long slender hooked bill grey-brown, and the legs and feet pink with darker webs. On losing the sooty-brown nestling down, the juvenile is all white below and dark brown above with buff edged wing-coverts. *In flight, the long thin neck which is fully extended, appears totally white from a distance,* the broad pointed wings flap rapidly and the tail is noticeably long. It is often seen in large flocks when fishing but may occasionally be seen singly. The nesting colonies are used for roosting during the winter. Flocks of immature birds have favoured gathering places on cliffs away from breeding colonies.

VOICE. It has several notes, mainly variations on a deep guttural 'kork' or 'kark'. At a large colony when nest-building is in progress in October, the noise can be deafening at close quarters.

FOOD. Mainly fish of various species including 'Rock-cod' (*Notothenia* sp.) and smelt. It also takes lobster-krill (probably *Munida* sp.) when shoals appear, and other crustaceans.

HABITAT, STATUS & BREEDING. A very common resident species, being found all round the coasts of the Falkland Is. It is a bird of the offshore waters and outer islands and rarely enters sheltered harbours where Rock Cormorants are most frequently seen. It breeds in large close-packed colonies, often inter-mingled with Rockhopper Penguins and sometimes with Black-browed Alba-trosses, usually on flat cliff-tops. Some nest on sloping cliff-sides, apparently where space on top is not available. Nest-building and renovation starts in

OVERLEAF King Cormorant in breeding plumage (October).

99

COLOUR ABOVE Giant Petrels at Slaughterhouse outlet, Stanley Harbour (*see p.* 80).

COLOUR BELOW Rock Cormorants at nests, Bold Point, East Falkland (*see p.* 97).

October and continues well into November. The nest is a column of mud, tussock-grass and pieces of seaweed about 1 ft. high, topped by a shallow cup lined with dry grass. Some eggs are laid at the end of October, but the majority are laid in the middle two weeks of November. The clutch is usually 3, but may be 2 or 4. The eggs are pale green-blue with limy encrustations. The nest column soon becomes plastered with droppings and in wet weather the ground between nests becomes a stinking quagmire. The eggs hatch during December and most of the juveniles are flying by mid-February.

DISTRIBUTION ABROAD. *Ph. albiventer* breeds on the eastern side of Tierra del Fuego, the Magellan Straits and Patagonia to 49°S, also on larger lakes in Neuquen and Rio Negro, Argentina (about 40°S). It ranges north on the Argentine coast to 35°S, occasionally reaching Uruguay. The range of the closely related *Ph. atriceps* overlaps with this species on islands south and west of Tierra del Fuego. It is distinguished by having mainly white cheeks, with their upper edge curved almost to the eye, instead of nearly horizontal across the cheeks as in *Ph. albiventer*. *Ph. atriceps* also has a white dorsal patch during the breeding-season, which *albiventer* never has. Other races of *Ph. albiventer* are found at the Crozets, Macquarie and Kerguelen Is.

White-necked Heron

Ardea cocoi Linn.   A. Garza mora   C. Garza cuca

IDENTIFICATION. Gigantic. c38″. A very large heron, almost twice the size of the resident Black-crowned Night Heron, it is *blue-grey above with black wing-tips; the head has a conspicuous black cap; the underparts are white with black streaks on the neck and black patches either side of the breast.* The juvenile lacks the black patches on the underparts but is streaked with buff. Its heavy, dagger-shaped yellow bill is about 6 in. long. Its *very long yellow legs* project far beyond the tail in flight.

HABITAT, STATUS & RECORDS. A very occasional visitor from South America that has been seen fishing up small streams in remote parts of the Falkland Is. It has been recorded at least three times in the past twenty years.

DISTRIBUTION ABROAD. Widely distributed throughout South America from the Guianas to about 42°S in Argentina; in Chile it is found from 25° to 47°S.

Black-crowned Night Heron on a rocky beach.

Common Egret

Casmerodius albus (Gmelin)   A. & C. Garza blanca

IDENTIFICATION. Immense. c34″. A *very large heron with all white plumage, very long black legs* that project well beyond the tail in flight, and a 4½ in., dagger-shaped, *yellow bill*. In summer it has a mantle of wispy feathers on the back which extends beyond the tips of the folded wings. It can only be confused with the Snowy Egret (*Egretta thula*, see Vagrants list) which is *much smaller*, about 20 in., has a *mainly black bill* and green and black legs.

HABITAT, STATUS & RECORDS. Recorded fishing along the beaches of sheltered inlets and up adjacent streams. Six certain records; two in October and the rest between April and June, all of single birds: October 1913 (Bennett, 1926); near Lake Hammond, West Falkland in mid-October 1958; on rocks at Cape Pembroke, 19th April 1960; at Fitzroy in late May 1960; one spent several weeks in June 1964 at Bluff Cove. One at Horseshoe Bay on 21st May 1959, was seen repeatedly in the same area in June, July and August and again on 6th December 1959, by Tony Nelson. It was very shy and sometimes associated with Kelp Gulls and Upland Geese on short grass.

DISTRIBUTION ABROAD. Widely distributed throughout South America and the southern United States, it breeds as far south as Santa Cruz (47°S) in Argentina, and is uncommon further south to Tierra del Fuego.

Black-crowned Night Heron

Nycticorax n. cyanocephalus (Molina)   A. Bruja   C. Huairavo común
Local name: Quawk

IDENTIFICATION. Medium-large. c21″. A fairly large, heavily-built shore-bird, easily recognized by its *predominantly grey wings, tail and underparts, black cap and back and long dagger-like greenish bill*. The adult is very handsomely marked dark grey and shiny black with a double or triple white plume at the nape, up to 8 in. long. The adult's legs are slaty in front and may be pink, yellow-green or orange-yellow behind with slaty toes and orange-yellow soles. Iris crimson. In juvenile and first year plumage it is equally distinctive, *being dark brown with heavy buff flecks above and buff streaked with dark brown below*, with orange iris and bright yellow-green legs. In second-year plumage it has a black cap, sometimes with short white plumes, a brown back with traces of slate-black, and buff

First-year Black-crowned Night Heron in Stanley harbour.

underparts lightly flecked with dark brown. The legs are pale green-yellow. In *flight* folds its neck back, giving it a thick-chested appearance, and flies with slow flaps of its broad rounded wings. The feet project just beyond the short tail. When flushed it almost invariably utters the typical harsh call from which the local name is derived. It is often seen resting motionless during the day or at high tide, but is active at dusk and later. Adults roost during autumn and winter in cypress trees at Carcass I. about 100 yds. from the beach, and they also roost in hulks where these are available.

VOICE. The usual note is a very harsh 'kwark' uttered when flushed and in flight; it often calls at night. A grunting note has also been noted and nestlings use a continuous ticking call.

FOOD. Feeds mainly on fish up to about 6 in. long and other small marine animals which it catches in rock pools at low tide. It also catches rats below the sea wall at Stanley. A number of pellets found at a resting place on Kidney I. on 28th October 1962, contained remains of two Grey-backed Storm-Petrels, many crickets and elytra of a beetle about 14 mm. long. The Storm-Petrel remains could have come from carcasses left by Short-eared Owls, or the Night Herons may have caught them as they clung to their nesting-hole entrances.

HABITAT, STATUS & BREEDING. A fairly common resident throughout the Falkland Is., although it is usually seen singly or in pairs. It is found on or near beaches, particularly those backed by cliffs and where there are rock pools at low tide; it also fishes up small streams, and is sometimes seen standing on kelp patches up to 500 yds. from the shore, where it probably catches small fish. It usually breeds communally, but single nests are not infrequently seen. Colonies of up to twenty-four pairs are known, but most are smaller. The nests are placed on steep low cliffs where growth of fachine, 'box' or tussock-grass clumps support them and they are built up as a flat platform with available sticks and grass. Colonies are also found nesting in thick beds of reeds or rushes in large ponds or lagoons, which may also be occupied by Brown-hooded Gulls. Lays 2, sometimes 3 or 4 smooth blue-green eggs. It is almost certainly sometimes double-brooded as eggs have been found between the end of October and late January. First clutches are probably laid between the end of October and mid-November, and second clutches laid from mid-December to mid-January.

DISTRIBUTION ABROAD. The race *N. n. cyanocephalus* is confined to the Falkland Is. Other races are found throughout most of South America from Brazil to Tierra del Fuego, also in North America, Asia, Europe and Africa.

Buff-necked Ibis

Theristicus caudatus melanopis (Gmelin)   A. & C. Bandurria común

IDENTIFICATION. Very large. c28″. A conspicuous, noisy but shy bird, about goose-size, with *a long down-curved black bill and orange head*, neck and breast, the latter with a grey band. It is generally grey mottled with dark brown above and has a black belly. Legs are long and dark red. Flies strongly on broad, long wings, showing black primaries, and a black tail. The call, a loud hard 'kwa-kwa' or 'clak-clak' uttered frequently in flight, carries a great distance and is easily recognized. The male and female are similar. The immature has a paler head than the adult, a grey back almost without dark markings and a shorter bill.

HABITAT, STATUS & RECORDS. In South America it is found both on swampy ground and ploughed land. In the Falkland Is. it has occurred at least nine times and has been seen on greens near settlements. Numbers varied from singles to parties up to seven. All the records fall in the two migration periods of March/April and October/November.

DISTRIBUTION ABROAD. *T. c. melanopis* is widespread on either side of the Andes from Tierra del Fuego north to 35°S in Argentina and to 27°S in Chile; it migrates northward from Tierra del Fuego for the winter. Another race, *T. c. caudatus* (breast and belly black), replaces this one in northern Argentina and is found as far north as Colombia and Venezuela. A third race, *T. c. branickii* (belly whitish), inhabits the Andes of northern Chile, Peru and Ecuador.

Coscoroba Swan

Coscoroba coscoroba (Molina)   A. Ganso blanco   C. Cisne coscoroba

IDENTIFICATION. Gigantic. c42″. Distinguished from the resident Black-necked Swan by its smaller size and *all white plumage* except for *black wing-tips*. *Bill crimson-red*; legs and feet pink.

HABITAT, STATUS & RECORDS. In the Falkland Is. it has been recorded on or near large ponds or by the shores of inlets. While there is no definite evidence, this species is said to have bred in Chartres camp years ago, and also near Mt. Pleasant in Fitzroy camp, where a pair were present throughout the summer of 1953. A small flock, less than ten, were seen flying towards Elephant Beach, Cape Dolphin early in February 1959. One was seen late in October 1952 at Beaver I., and another in December 1954 at New I. Two, one an immature, spent eight weeks between July and September 1951 on floodwater east of Stanley.

DISTRIBUTION ABROAD. Breeds in the southern parts of Argentina and Chile from Tierra del Fuego to 45°S in Chile and to Paraguay and southeast Brazil. Migrates north in winter to about 25°S.

Black-necked Swan

Cygnus melancoryphus (Molina)   A. & C. Cisne cuello negro
Local name: Swan

IDENTIFICATION. Gigantic. c48″. This is the largest breeding waterbird in the Falkland Is. It is immediately recognized by its *great size and all white plumage, apart from the black head and neck*. In flight shows the typical silhouette of heavy body, broad wings and very long black neck extended fully. On the rare occasions when a close approach is possible, a white streak curving back from the bill through the eye is noticeable. The bill is pale blue-grey with a variable red basal knob, much larger on the male than the female. The legs and feet are flesh-coloured. Juvenile and immature birds resemble the adult but appear greyish or buffish white from a distance. It is a very wary bird with strong flight, and often flies when intruders are a quarter of a mile away or more. All the flight feathers are moulted in late February and early March and until new feathers have grown the bird cannot fly.

VOICE. It has a loud plaintive whinnying note, 'whee-her-her-her-her' (uttered with the head thrown up), which carries a long way. The male also has a musical call, 'hooee-hoo-hoo'.

FOOD. The bulk of the diet is water-weed obtained in creeks and estuaries from underwater rocks. It also takes various water insects.

HABITAT, STATUS & BREEDING. A resident species but not numerous, it is found mainly on East Falkland, especially in Lafonia and the adjacent islands, but it has bred recently near Fox Bay on West Falkland. Winter flocks up to seventy strong gather at a few tidal estuaries or creeks, including Swan Inlet, Lafonia and the Murrel estuary northwest of Stanley. Flocks are found between early March and November in these places, but those seen together after September are almost certainly non-breeding birds. Immigration from South America has been suspected and the following observation by R. Reid on George I. may support this suggestion. On 2nd November 1961, between 19.30 and 20.00 hrs. local time, twenty swans flew in a northerly direction between George and Barren Is., disappearing towards the East Falkland mainland. All of these birds were in pairs, and all but two pairs were separated from the next by at least a quarter of a mile. It nests between early August and mid-September, building a large nest of diddle-dee twigs and grass on an islet in a pond or close to a lake. 4–7 cream coloured eggs are laid.

DISTRIBUTION ABROAD. Found in southeastern Brazil, Uruguay, Paraguay, Argentina except the northwest, and Chile from 30°S to Tierra del Fuego. It breeds mainly in the southern parts of Chile and Argentina from Tierra del Fuego to about 42°S.

Ashy-headed Goose

Chloëphaga poliocephala Sclater   A. Avutarda cabeza gris   C. Canquén
Local names: Coast Brant, White-breasted Brant

IDENTIFICATION. Large. c24″. This goose is slightly larger than the Ruddy-headed and may be distinguished by its *grey head and neck*, *chestnut breast* and mantle which are lightly barred with black, its *white belly* and barred black and white flanks. The lower part of the back is grey-brown and the rump and tail are black. The male and female are similarly coloured. The bill is black and the legs are orange behind and on the outside, black in front and on the inside. The webs and toes are also black and the soles are orange (*see also* Table 3).

HABITAT, STATUS & RECORDS. A rare species that has been recorded at most times of the year, it is most likely to occur with Upland and Ruddy-headed Geese in their usual habitat of well-watered short grass, but has only been seen in very small numbers. It has bred at Spring Point, Roy Cove and New I. in recent years and has probably also bred on the East mainland. In Chile it lays 4–6 eggs in a grass nest lined with down; the breeding season in the Falkland Is. would probably be October–November.

DISTRIBUTION ABROAD. A widely distributed bird in southern Chile and southern Argentina, it breeds in the Andes from 37–42°S in Chile and from 37–53°S in Argentina, also in the lowlands, islands and Andes of Chile from 42–55°S. It is scarce in Tierra del Fuego, being replaced mainly by *Ch. picta* and *Ch. rubidiceps*. It is migratory; the first immigrants reach Tierra del Fuego during September, and its winter range extends to 35°S in Argentina and Chile.

Ruddy-headed Goose

Chloëphaga rubidiceps Sclater   A. & C. Avutarda colorada
Local names: Brent, Brant

IDENTIFICATION. Medium-large. 20–22″. Resembles the female Upland Goose, but separated by its *smaller size, brighter chestnut head and neck* with a white eye-ring, all brown and black, barred breast and flanks, *bright chestnut belly and under tail-coverts*. When swimming, the rich chestnut under tail-coverts are particularly noticeable as the tail is well elevated. The male and female are alike, but the male is larger and has a brighter coloured head and neck. The legs are brighter orange than the female Upland's, and are sometimes spotted with black. The bill is black. It is commonly seen with Upland Geese when its smaller size is quite obvious if colour differences cannot be seen (*see* Table 3). Large flocks of both species are seen in parts of the Falkland Is., but this species is less common and decidedly more shy. A moult of all flight feathers, known locally as 'shedding' takes place in late December and early January. Individuals with a variable amount of white on the belly are seen sometimes; these may have arisen through hybridization with the Ashy-headed Goose, or they may be the result of mutation.

TABLE 3. *Recognition of 'Chloephaga' Geese in Flight*

Species	Size	Head	Rump	Tail	Under Tail-Covs.	Wings
KELP Ad. Male	Very large	White	White	White	White	White
Imm. Male	Very large	White	White	White	White	Variable black sec. covs. and primaries
Ad. Female	Large	Black	White	White	White	
Imm. Female	Large	Black	Black	White	White	All have the same black and white wing pattern
UPLAND Ad. Male	Very large	White	White	White but black centre	White	
Imm. Male	Very large	Greyish	White	Black	White	
Female	Very large	Red-brown	Black	Black	Grey-brown	There are only minor colour differences between species
RUDDY-HEADED Male and Female	Medium-large	Richer red-brown	Black	Black	Chestnut	
ASHY-HEADED Male and Female	Large	Pale grey	Black	Black	Chestnut	

VOICE. The female is more vocal than the male, and often uses a distinctive short rasping quacking note before flight and when flying. The male has a short 'seep' whistle, similar to that of the male Kelp Goose but more harsh in tone: it is often used as a pre-flight call. The male also has a very low-pitched grunt. A party of four birds watched swimming on a pond at mid-winter uttered a mellow, quiet, double whistle, 'peeo-waoo'.

FOOD. It feeds mainly on the short, green grass found by ponds and around settlements.

HABITAT, STATUS & BREEDING. A resident that is generally distributed round the two main islands and on outlying islands. It is very numerous only in parts of West Falkland and appears to be more restricted to coastal areas of fine grass than the Upland. It nests from late September to early November, laying 5–8 cream coloured eggs in a nest of grass lined with down. The nests are usually well hidden amongst long grass or rushes, beneath overhanging rock outcrops or even inside old Magellanic Penguin burrows. The female alone incubates while the male 'waits off' by the nearest pond, often at a considerable distance from the nest.

DISTRIBUTION ABROAD. *Ch. rubidiceps* breeds only in Tierra del Fuego and in smaller numbers in extreme southern Chile and Argentina to about 52°S. It is migratory, and in winter reaches about 37°S in Argentina. There is no evidence of migration to or from the Falkland Is., but it is a summer visitor to Tierra del Fuego, arriving in September and leaving in March and April. It is possible that there is some interchange between these two populations.

Upland Goose

Chloëphaga picta leucoptera (Gmelin)   A. Cauquén   C. Caiquén

IDENTIFICATION. Very large. 29–30″. A large, unusually tame goose, which is familiar to all Falkland islanders. The *male* looks mainly white from a distance, but the *long black legs and feet with noticeable white 'trousers'* distinguish it from the male Kelp Goose. The male's head and underparts are white, barred with black on flanks and shoulders; the back is grey-brown and the rump and tail are white, but the tail has a variable number of black feathers in the centre. The *female* is slightly smaller and looks dark from a distance. It has a rich, rusty-brown head and neck; breast and belly are barred black and brown, while *the flanks are barred black and white*; under tail-coverts are black, the back grey-brown and the legs are orange or dark yellow. Both male and female have black bills. The *immature male* has a grey shade on the head and neck, variable black barring on the underparts and a mainly black tail. The *immature female* is duller than the adult, with orange-brown legs. In flight the male appears mainly white with black and white wings. The female is easily separated from the female Kelp Goose by her *all black tail*, but the only distinctions from the Ruddy-headed Goose are her larger size, *black under tail-coverts* and less ruddy colour beneath (*see* Table 3). It is frequently seen in parties and flocks up to about a hundred strong. The adults moult all their flight feathers towards the end of December, and at that period and when the young are still incapable of flight they take to the water of ponds or the sea when disturbed. Pairs are strongly territorial when nesting.

Upland Geese on coastal grass near Bluff Cove.

VOICE. The male's usual call is a weak whistle 'wheep'. The female commonly utters a low rattling 'a-rrrrr' in flight and on the ground; she also has a short low grunting call.

FOOD. During the spring and summer feeds mainly on short green grass, for which it is disliked by some sheep farmers. In a sandy or peaty soil where the grass grows thinly, it is pulled out by the roots. It also commonly eats berries of diddle-dee, tea-berry and wild strawberry during late summer and autumn. At these seasons an Upland Goose is considered at its best for human consumption. It can be found on beaches in hard frosts or when the grass is snow-covered.

HABITAT, STATUS & BREEDING. It is usually found within a mile of salt water, particularly on greens near settlements and ponds and around creeks. It is numerous and widely dstributed on the larger islands and mainland coastal regions, but is comparatively rare within a radius of 5–10 miles of Stanley due to shooting for food. It lays 5–8 large cream-coloured eggs in a grass or twig nest lined with down amongst fern, diddle-dee or white grass. The main season for eggs is mid-September to late October, but eggs have been found from early August to late November. The female alone incubates while the male 'waits off', usually near the nest. Skuas and Kelp Gulls take many small goslings, even though the parents defend their young vigorously.

DISTRIBUTION ABROAD. The race *Ch. p. leucoptera* is restricted to the Falkland Is. A smaller race, *Ch. p. p.* is found in southern South America from Tierra del Fuego to 35°S in Chile and to 38°S in Argentina. It migrates north to about 35°S in Argentina in winter.

Kelp Goose

Chloëphaga hybrida malvinarum Philippi   A. Avutarda blanca   C. Caranca

IDENTIFICATION. Male, very large c29″; female, large c26″. The *adult male* with its *totally white plumage* is the most conspicuous bird of the rocky shores and is unmistakable, except at long distances, when it can be confused with the Sheathbill. (The Sheathbill's movements, e.g. walking, running and wing-beats are much quicker.) The male has *stout, bright yellow legs and feet* and short, deep black bill with a pink patch on the culmen. The *female* is less conspicuous and can easily be overlooked having heavily *barred black and white neck, breast and flanks, dark brown back and head* with a white eye-ring and a light brown cap; the rump, tail, under tail-coverts and belly are white. The white carpal joint often shows as a bar on the side (*see* Table 3 for separation in flight from female Upland). The female has bright yellow legs and *a pink bill*. The *juvenile male* has a sooty head and neck with white forehead, lores and eyestripe, a black bill, mainly black scapulars and back, dark brown secondary coverts, dark primaries and some black bars on the neck and flanks. These dark feathers are lost gradually and by September, a first year male can be recognized by its remaining dark secondary coverts and primaries. Most of the dark wing feathers are lost by March, although some dark primaries or secondary coverts may be retained till the following November. The *immature female* resembles the adult but lacks the light brown cap, has dark upper tail-coverts at first and a dull yellowish bill. The immature male and female both have dull greenish-yellow legs and feet. (*See* Table 3.) The pairs remain together throughout the year and family groups are maintained until mid-winter at least. Small flocks, but sometimes as many as a hundred, are seen in late winter and early spring, when much chasing and displaying takes place. Displaying is seen from September to late November, but birds in flocks after late October are probably all non-breeders, and in January include failed breeders. Adults moult their flight feathers in December; a party of thirty apparently flightless birds seen on 6th January

Falkland Kelp Geese; a pair displaying.

1963, took to the open sea at Seal Point, south of Stanley, rather than attempting to fly. The flight appears somewhat laboured and is usually only a few feet above the water. It can swim well but only takes to the water when chased along a beach, when escorting flightless young or during the moult of flight feathers. (Colour photo: p. 102)

VOICE. The pre-flight and flight call of the male is a thin weak whistle, 'si-si-si'; that of the female is a loud low honk, 'arnk-arnk'. In communal displays the male utters a higher-pitched wheezy 'wheee' and a rapid repetition of the 'si-si-si' note. The female utters a loud 'ooer' or 'ooeroo' with the neck held high.

FOOD. It feeds largely on the bright green papery 'Sea lettuce' (*Ulva* sp.), which is abundant in the intertidal zone of boulder and shingle beaches. It also eats a type of Red Alga of similar form, but smaller (*Porphyra* sp.) which is found in the same zone of boulder beaches. During the autumn it sometimes wanders away from the shore to eat ripe diddle-dee berries, and it has been seen grazing short green grass.

HABITAT, STATUS & BREEDING. A resident that is fairly common and widely distributed around the Falkland Is., it is almost restricted to rocky coasts and shingle beaches, but it visits nearby freshwater ponds for bathing and drinking. It nests in late October and early November, laying 4–6 eggs, occasionally 7, of a light buff colour, in a rough grass nest, which is well lined with down when the clutch is complete. The nest is near the shore sheltered amongst tussock clumps, sometimes on a ledge of a low cliff. The female alone incubates while the male stands guard close by. Several males in first year plumage have been seen apparently paired with females as early as 30th August, but they do not breed until they are at least two years old. Most pairs breeding on Kidney I. leave between late March and mid-April and migrate to sheltered mainland bays and creeks around Stanley for the winter, returning to Kidney I. in September and October. One adult female, colour-banded in Stanley harbour on 10th May 1957 was found nesting on Kidney I. in December 1958, November 1960 and November 1962. It was seen each winter from 1957 to 1963 on various dates between 1st March and 17th September on the south shore of Stanley harbour, between 300 yds. west and 1,200 yds. east of the place where it was originally trapped.

DISTRIBUTION ABROAD. The race *Ch. h. malvinarum* is confined to the Falkland Is. A smaller race, *Ch. h. h.* is abundant on the coasts and islands of Chile from 42°S to Tierra del Fuego and less common on the Atlantic coast to about 50°S. It occasionally wanders north as far as 33°S in Chile and 39°S in Argentina.

Patagonian Crested Duck

Lophonetta s. specularioides (King)   A. Pato crestón   C. Pato juarjual del Sur
Local name: Grey Duck

IDENTIFICATION. Medium-large. 20–22″. This large duck is recognized by its *mottled brown and buff underparts*, whitish face and neck contrasting with *a dark brown patch encircling the eye and extending to the nape*, and its *long pointed black tail and black under tail-coverts*. The back is dark brown. It may be identified even at a considerable distance by its distinctive silhouette of a long body, a slender neck and small head, with the long tail cocked up. A ragged crest which falls from the nape is not conspicuous except on a close view. The bill is mainly black above and yellowish below. The iris colour varies between bright crimson and brick-red; the legs and feet are dark grey. The male is larger than the female and more brightly coloured. The juvenile resembles the adult but the face and neck are light brown. In *flight* it appears uniform brown above and lighter below, but it is easily recognized by its *black speculum glossed with bronze*, and *white tips to the secondaries*. It is commonly seen in pairs, trios and small parties; flocks up to thirty-five have been recorded in creeks. It is an aggressive bird and strongly territorial; it will attack others of its own and different species. (Colour photo: p. 119)

VOICE. It is a rather noisy bird. A call frequently heard, that of the male, is a buzzy 'sheeoo'. The usual call of the female is a low grating 'querk'. When feeding at night uses a quiet nasal 'quek-quek-quek . . .' repeated rapidly, and also a long-drawn 'que-ek'. The juvenile has a rapidly repeated 'see-see-see' and a quick low rattling call.

FOOD. There are few actual records of food, but it probably feeds mainly on small crustaceans which it obtains by dabbling and sieving liquid mud in creeks when the tide is low. It has also been recorded up-ending, apparently eating a fine green alga found in rock pools and taking waste matter at a sewer outlet. It also drinks and bathes where fresh-water streams flow onto beaches.

HABITAT, STATUS & BREEDING. It is most often seen on salt water, either on the sea in sheltered bays or in creeks; also on ponds near the sea. It is a common resident, well distributed around the Falkland Is., but probably more common around West Falkland. It is uncommon near Stanley. Territories are probably held throughout the year. 1,400 yds. of mixed coastline at George I. (mostly rocks, but 300 yds. of sand beach) carried eight pairs in late August 1961 (R. Reid). The breeding season is very extended; eggs or very young ducklings have been seen in every month from mid-July to early May, but the main breeding season is September to November; it is often double-brooded. The nest is made of dry grass, diddle-dee strands or small fern, lined with down amongst grass, tussock-grass, diddle-dee or fern. It may be close to water but is often well inland. Lays 5–7 cream coloured eggs, but clutches of 9 and 11 have been known.

DISTRIBUTION ABROAD. *L. s. s.* is widely distributed in two distinct regions of South America. It is found in the Andes from 36°S in Chile and from 38°S in Argentina to Tierra del Fuego. It occupies coastal parts of Chile from 45°S and of Argentina from 42°S to Tierra del Fuego. It ranges north in winter to 37°S on the coast of Argentina. A larger race, *L. s. alticola*, occupies the Andes of Peru, Bolivia, Chile (to 35°S) and Argentina (to 38°S).

Falkland Flightless Steamer Duck

Tachyeres brachypterus (Latham)   A. Pato vapor malvinero   C. Not recorded
Local names: Logger, Loggerhead

IDENTIFICATION. Male, very large, c29″. Female, large, c24″. One of the most familiar Falkland shorebirds, it is easily recognized by its *extremely heavy body, large rounded head and broad strong bill*. It swims fairly low in the water, sometimes with its back almost awash, *showing a diagonal white wing-patch* and carrying its short pointed tail flat, but holding it erect and fanned when displaying. Both male and female have a scaly pattern of slate-grey feathers edged with blackish and red-brown on the back, sides of the breast and flanks; the breast is similarly patterned with dark and red-brown and contrasts sharply with the white belly and under tail-coverts. The *adult male* is larger than the female, has a *variable grey and white head* and hind neck and a red-brown patch on the throat and cheeks. Old males have an almost completely white head, while younger males have a grey head with white round the eye continuing in a curve down the side of the neck, separating the grey nape from the red-brown cheeks. The *bill* of the male is *bright orange* with a large black nail. *The female* has a *dark brown head* with a white eye-ring and a *narrow white line* curving from the eye down the side of the head, and the *bill* is a variable *green-yellow*. Both male and female have orange-yellow legs and feet. The juvenile and first year plumage resembles that of the female, but usually lacks the white head streak. The immature bird has pale yellow legs and feet with blackish ankle and toe joints. From the second year, an immature male gradually gains more grey on the head and more orange on the bill. Although the 'Logger' is incapable of sustained flight in the

ABOVE Patagonian Crested Ducks at Bertha's Beach (*see p.* 117).
BELOW Adult male Falkland Flightless Steamer Duck ('Logger') at Watt Cove, East Falkland.

normal manner, it is expert at swimming and diving and makes full use of its disproportionately short wings. Whenever it wishes to move quickly, to escape from danger or chase away an intruder, it 'steams' rapidly over the water, often for 50 yds. or more, kicking up a great deal of spray with the combined action of rapid wing-beats and hard paddling with its large feet, while the breast ploughs the water like the bows of a boat. In a very strong wind the whole body may be lifted clear, but it cannot travel more than a few yards in this way. A female flushed from rocks at Eliza Cove in mid-July 1959, in a strong northwesterly averaging 30 kts., gusting 40 kts., became airborne straight from the rocks and travelled 12–15 ft. about a foot above rocks and water. A method of attack, which is particularly effective against swimming Kelp Gulls, involves extending and lowering the head and bill till they plough the water and then gradually submerging itself with hardly a ripple as it swims towards the intruder. An interval of a few seconds calm follows, then the 'Logger' surfaces with a splash almost under the surprised gull, which leaves in a hurry. Flocks of immature birds are seen throughout the year, but are largest in autumn and winter. They keep together and feed communally in deep water, all diving within a few seconds of each other. A large flock of up to 200 immature birds and some apparently-adult males, gathers on the sand beach at Surf Bay well before dusk and then marches across it to a freshwater pond behind the beach. Here they drink, splash and preen and are generally noisy until they settle down to roost, probably on the banks of the pond. Pairs with small ducklings will roost on a beach just above high water mark. It is very fond of drinking fresh water, which it obtains from streams where they enter the sea, or from ponds.

VOICE. It is a noisy bird and can often be heard calling at night, particularly the male, whose loud vibratory alarm call, 'cheeroo', carries a great distance. A quieter, more conversational call of the male, 'cheeoo', is often heard, also a rapid sharp 'kek-kek-kek'. The female has a short, guttural quacking note, and when displaying or disturbed utters a peculiar low creaking note, with the head thrown up vertically.

FOOD. It takes mainly shellfish including mussels, limpets, and various bivalves, also crabs and many other small marine animals. It also takes offal occasionally and tamed birds will readily eat whole corn (maize) as fed to domestic fowls. It obtains its food by up-ending in shallow water, or by diving in deep water, each dive being of about 30 seconds' duration.

HABITAT, STATUS & BREEDING. A very common and widespread species throughout the Falkland Is., it is found especially where there are large offshore kelp beds, and is numerous in sheltered harbours and creeks. It is a strongly

ABOVE A pair of Chiloë Wigeon flying over Bertha's Beach Pond (*see p.* 125). 121
CENTRE Silver Teal on Bertha's Beach Pond (Speckled Teal at side) (*see p.* 127).
BELOW Adult Turkey Vulture (*see p.* 129).

territorial bird; pairs defend their own stretch of beach and adjoining water against intrusion from neighbouring pairs and other species throughout the year. It is almost always on salt water during daylight, but has been seen on ponds near the sea during the day. It ranges regularly to the outer edge of kelp beds and has been observed 3 miles offshore. It nests in grass, dry kelp, diddle-dee or tussock-grass, sometimes in old Magellanic Penguin burrows, usually within 200 yds. of a beach, but sometimes a quarter of a mile from the sea. The nest is a depression scantily filled with available grasses or fibres and lined with down. It lays 5–8 large buff eggs, rarely, 10 or more; one brood of 12 ducklings is recorded. The female alone incubates while the male patrols his territory. The main laying season is from mid-September to December, but nests with eggs have been found in all months of the year. Mortality among newly-hatched ducklings is high; one brood of 7 at Kidney I. diminished to 4 in five days. Kelp Gulls and Skuas attack ducklings and Giant Petrels probably do so, but full-grown birds have no natural predators except seals.

DISTRIBUTION ABROAD. This species is only found in the Falkland Is. A similar flightless Steamer Duck, *T. pteneres* is found on the coast of Chile from 37°S to islands south of Tierra del Fuego, and on the coast of Argentina from about 42°S to Tierra del Fuego and Staten I.

Flying Steamer Duck

Tachyeres patachonicus (King)
A. Pato vapor volador   C. Pato quetro volador
Local name: Canvasback

IDENTIFICATION. Male, very large, c28″. Female, medium-large, c23″. Closely resembles the 'Logger' in general colouration, but it can be recognized by its more slender build, *much less heavy bill and considerably longer wings*. It is, nevertheless, very difficult to separate from the 'Logger' when swimming. In flight it is easily identified by its *large size and dark plumage generally, with a white belly and a large white speculum on the secondaries*. The male is larger than the female. It is much more shy than the 'Logger', but it also has the habit of 'steaming', although it tends to rise further off the water. It flies well but often seems reluctant to fly far and will land again within a few hundred yards.

VOICE. There are apparently no published notes on its calls. In contrast to the 'Logger', it does not appear to be a vigorous defender of territory.

FOOD. No records from the Falkland Is. are available, but in South America it apparently takes fewer bivalves and more crustaceans than the local flightless species.

HABITAT, STATUS & BREEDING. It is found both on freshwater ponds and the sea, but is much more frequently seen on ponds *during the day* than the 'Logger'. Although apparently well distributed, its true status is unknown due to continuing confusion with the previous species, but it is probably now an uncommon breeding duck. It nests from October, possibly earlier, laying 5–8 buff eggs, which are smaller than the 'Logger's', in a nest closely resembling that of the 'Logger'.

DISTRIBUTION ABROAD. This species inhabits both inland waters and rivers, as well as the coasts of southern South America. It is found from 37°S in Chile and on the Pacific coast, and about 44°S on the coast of Argentina to Tierra del Fuego and Staten I. It is also found inland in Argentina as far north as 38°S.

Speckled Teal

Anas flavirostris Vieillot   A. Pato barcino   C. Pato jergón chico
Local names: Teal, Duck

IDENTIFICATION. Small-medium. c15″. The *smallest duck breeding in the Falkland Is.*, it is recognized by its small size and *bright yellow sides to its bill*. The

Falkland Flightless Steamer Duck; a pair with ducklings.   123

Speckled Teal on a pond at Carcass Island.

plumage looks generally light grey-brown from a distance, but is actually streaked buff on dark brown above and spotted brown on buff on the breast. The head is noticeably the darkest part with a slanting darker streak through the eye. The male and female are similarly coloured, but the latter is duller and slightly smaller. The legs and feet are blue-grey. When swimming, it has a characteristic down-at-the-front attitude. In flight it is recognized by its small size and *dark appearance with no marked head pattern*. The speculum is black partly glossed with green, with narrow buff stripes fore and aft, but only the rear stripe is easily visible. It flies very rapidly in close groups. It is not usually seen singly and may be seen in large flocks up to 200 strong, especially in autumn and winter. *It is notably more tame than other Falkland ducks*. Moult of the flight feathers takes place in December, when flocks gather on ponds with other ducks.

VOICE. The call of the male, often heard from flocks, is a short, musical trill. The female has a high-pitched, quacking call.

FOOD. Few records of food are available, but it has been watched swimming rapidly with the head held low and the bill half under water, presumably straining minute animals or weed fragments. It has also been recorded diving, each dive being of about 5 seconds' duration. In winter it sometimes eats berries of 'pig-vine'.

HABITAT, STATUS & BREEDING. A very widespread and numerous resident that is found throughout the Falkland Is., but is probably more numerous on East Falkland, where there are more ponds with water-weed. It has a wide choice of habitat, being found on the smallest ponds and streams as well as on large lakes with other ducks, in creeks and on the waters of sheltered coves. The breeding season is extended, and two broods are usually reared. It nests from mid-August onwards, laying 5–8 reddish-cream eggs in a well-hidden grass nest, which may be near water or up to a mile from a pond. A brood of young ducklings has been seen as late as April. One of a brood of 3 non-flying juveniles was banded by a pond on Cape Pembroke on 11th January 1961, and it was shot at the same pond about 25th June 1961.

DISTRIBUTION ABROAD. This race, *A. f. f.*, is widespread in the southern part of South America, from Tierra del Fuego, where it is a summer visitor arriving about the end of September, to about 30°S in Chile and Argentina. In Chile it is more common from about 39°S to Tierra del Fuego. It migrates northward in winter and is also found in southeastern Brazil, Paraguay and Uruguay. Three other races are found in the Andean regions of South America.

Chiloë Wigeon

Anas sibilatrix Poeppig   A. Pato overo   C. Pato real
Local names: Black and White Wigeon, Wigeon

IDENTIFICATION. Medium-large. c20″. This fairly large duck has a *conspicuously pied head*; the fore-part of the face is white, the rest of the head and neck are black with a bottle-green sheen on the side of the head. *The whole bird appears very dark* unless seen at close range. The breast is closely barred black and white; the belly is white with a variable amount of orange on the flanks, but this colour is not easily seen in the field. *The back and scapulars are black with white streaks on the scapulars*. The bill is pale blue-grey tipped with black; the legs and feet are black. The male and female are similar, but the female has less white on the head and is smaller. It is easily identified in flight by *a large crescentic white patch on each forewing* and *its white rump* contrasting with the dark upperparts and tail. The speculum is velvet-black but it is not conspicuous. The immature lacks the white on the head. It is usually seen in pairs or small groups, alone or with Teal species and sometimes in flocks of thirty or forty in autumn and winter. (Colour photo: p. 120)

VOICE. The alarm call is a soft whistling 'huweet'. It often calls when feeding at night. A rapid chattering whistle, short quacking notes and trilling notes were heard from a small party in flight on 20th October, accompanied by an aerial display when one bird repeatedly tipped up its head towards another that it was following.

FOOD. Few records of its feeding habits have been made, but it has been noted dabbling amongst thick weed in a pond. It also grazes short grass round ponds and settlements, and often grazes during the night in grass and clover paddocks round Bleaker I. settlement in October. A very tame individual associated with domestic ducks round the settlement paddocks on West Point I. in November 1962.

HABITAT, STATUS & BREEDING. A resident that may be seen in most parts of the Falkland Is. although nowhere very common, it is locally numerous in parts of Lafonia and apparently rare on West Falkland. It is found on rivers, large ponds or lakes and on green pasture near the shore, also less frequently in offshore kelp patches. Nests can be found between September and late December and it may be double-brooded. 5–8 white eggs are laid in a grass nest, which is well hidden and often a long way from the nearest water.

DISTRIBUTION ABROAD. One of the commonest ducks in Chile, it breeds from 28°S to Tierra del Fuego, where it is a summer resident arriving in October. It is resident in central Chile, but is more common from 40°S to Tierra del Fuego. It also breeds in Argentina from 34°S to Tierra del Fuego and migrates north in winter. It does not occur in the Andean regions, but is also found in southeastern Brazil, Paraguay and Uruguay.

Yellow-billed Pintail

Anas georgica Vieillot   A. Pato maicero   C. Pato jergón grande
Local names: Grey Teal, Coast Teal

IDENTIFICATION. Medium-large. c20″. This species resembles the Speckled Teal in general colouration but is *much larger*, about the same size as the Chiloë Wigeon. The main differences are that *the head is noticeably rounded and the neck is rather long and slender*; both head and neck appear nearly uniform light brown from a distance, but the crown has a broad dark red-brown central stripe. *The bill is fairly long with yellow-ochre sides* and a black culmen stripe. *The back is dark brown well streaked with buff*; the breast is more rufous spotted with dark brown. The male and female are similarly coloured, but the female has a paler yellow bill and a lighter neck and is also slightly smaller. The legs and feet are dark grey. In flight, its larger size, light head and longer bill, grey-brown shoulder and a *whitish patch on the belly* distinguish it from the Speckled Teal. The brown tail is somewhat elongated and pointed, but is not often noticeable. The wing pattern above is mainly brown with a green or bronze glossed black speculum, conspicuously bordered fore and aft with buff. The juvenile has a duller bill and a greyer breast.

VOICE. It seems to be rather a silent bird. The only call noted is a harsh, guttural quack, uttered by a female when anxious about her brood.

FOOD. There are no records available of food taken in the Falkland Is., but in Chile it takes aquatic plants and small aquatic animals.

HABITAT, STATUS & BREEDING. It is usually found on freshwater ponds with other ducks, but has also been recorded on salt water in a sheltered bay. It is one of the least common Falkland ducks, although it is well distributed and said to be locally numerous in parts of Lafonia. It may be more common than is supposed because, (a) it can be mistaken for the abundant Speckled Teal and (b) a few breed successfully within easy reach of Stanley, where all edible ducks are in danger of being shot. There is a possibility that it is migratory and leaves the Islands in autumn; all personal records are of birds seen between September and March, but Abbott reported in 1861 that it was resident all the year. It nests between September and December and is probably double-brooded. It lays 7–10 cream coloured eggs in a grass nest lined with down hidden amongst coarse grass or rushes, or amongst small tussock-grass.

DISTRIBUTION ABROAD. This is the most common duck in Chile and Argentina. It is a summer visitor to Tierra del Fuego, arriving there at the start of spring. It ranges north throughout Chile to Peru, occasionally reaching Ecuador; on the east side of the Andes it breeds mainly in the southern two-thirds of Argentina and ranges north in winter to Uruguay, Paraguay, southern Brazil and Bolivia.

Silver Teal

Anas versicolor fretensis King
A. Pato argentino   C. Pato capuchino austral
Local name: Pampa Teal

IDENTIFICATION. Medium. c17″. This duck is slightly larger than the Speckled Teal. The most striking features, by which it may be recognized at long distances are the *wide dark brown cap* (including the eye) *which contrasts sharply with the pale cream cheeks,* and the *rather long and deep pale blue bill* with an orange basal patch. The breast is buff spotted with brown and the flanks are strongly barred with black and white. The rump and tail appear silver-grey from a distance, but are actually finely barred black and white. The back and wings are mainly dark brown, the long scapulars streaked buff and dark brown.

The legs are grey. The male and female are similar, but the male is generally brighter coloured. In flight it shows a grey-brown shoulder and a broad *glossy blue-green speculum on the secondaries bordered fore and aft with equal white lines. The underwing is white with a dark brown leading edge.* It is seen singly and in groups, often in association with Speckled Teal and Chiloë Wigeon, but it is rather shy. (Colour photo: p. 120)

VOICE. The usual call is a high-pitched whistle 'weeoo', but it is not noisy. A distinctive descending, rattling call was heard from an adult suspected of having hidden young.

FOOD. It has been observed up-ending and dabbling with the head and neck below the surface, probably eating water-weed, but apparently no records exist of the food taken by this species.

HABITAT, STATUS & BREEDING. It frequents freshwater ponds on both East and West Falkland, where it is seen in small numbers, although it is locally numerous, and small flocks are seen in winter. There is no available information on breeding in South America or the Falkland Is., except that a pair seen on 20th January 1963 on a large pond in Island Harbour camp, probably had young hidden in thick rushes.

DISTRIBUTION ABROAD. The race *A. v. fretensis* is found in southern Chile from 42°S and southern Argentina from about 40°S to Tierra del Fuego. It is a summer visitor to Tierra del Fuego where it arrives about the middle of September. A smaller darker race, *A. v. v.*, is found in southern Brazil, southern Bolivia, Paraguay, Uruguay and Chile from 33°S to 42°S and in Argentina from the north to about 38°S. Both races migrate north in Argentina in the winter.

Cinnamon Teal

Anas cyanoptera Vieillot   A. & C. Pato colorado
Local name: Red Teal

IDENTIFICATION. Medium. c18″. The adult male in full plumage is unmistakable; it has *all the face, neck and underparts a rich glossy chestnut*, a black crown, blackish-brown back with long buff stripes and *black under tail-coverts*. Both male and female have a *fairly long black bill and yellow legs*. The male moults to an 'eclipse' plumage resembling the female for about three months in summer (December–February?). The female and eclipse male are mainly light brown on head, neck and underparts, flecked with dark brown, and are easily confused with the Yellow-billed Pintail and Speckled Teal when at rest. The black bill and the male's black under tail-coverts are the best distinguishing features. Both sexes in flight are recognized by their black primaries, *pale blue forewing, and a white line separating it from a glossy green speculum on the secondaries*. When feeding it up-ends in shallow water to collect water-weed and also dives frequently.

HABITAT, STATUS & RECORDS. This is a very rare bird in the Falkland Is.; no information on its breeding in the Islands is available apart from the fact that it has bred at one place on West Falkland, and is reputed to breed still at Bull Point in Lafonia. It is most likely to be seen on ponds with other Teal, Pintail and Chiloë Wigeon. Whether it is a migrant or resident in the Falkland Is. is unknown.

DISTRIBUTION ABROAD. The race *A. c. c.* is fairly common in Chile from 27°S to 48°S, but is uncommon further south towards Tierra del Fuego. It is widespread also throughout most of Argentina except the northwest, southern Peru, Brazil, Uruguay and Paraguay. Other races are found north to Mexico, the United States and southwestern Canada.

Turkey Vulture

Cathartes aura falklandica (Sharpe)   A. Cuervo cabeza roja   C. Gallinazo
Local names: Turkey Buzzard, Turkey

IDENTIFICATION. Large. c26″. Wingspan: 5′2″, 5′7″ (two specimens). *A large dark blackish-brown bird* with bare bright red head and foreneck, it is easily recognized by its leisurely flight, with *slow flapping, very broad, long wings, conspicuously fingered*. It glides with the wings raised about 30° above horizontal, with *a typical wavering, rocking action*. The head looks very small and the *tail is quite long and slightly graduated*. When overhead it shows dark body plumage and under wing-coverts contrasting with pale grey undersides to the flight feathers. The bill is creamy-white and very strongly hooked. The legs and feet are dull greyish-crimson. On the ground it appears very bulky, has a peculiar waddling gait and shows light buff edges to the secondaries. The juvenile has a dull grey head, dark bill, dull brownish legs and, for a few weeks after fledging, a collar of whitish down. The immature bird does not gain the red head and pale bill until it is more than a year old. It hunts singly and in small parties, but numbers gather where food is plentiful, over their nesting islands and after the breeding season. It is usually comparatively tame, but where it is persecuted becomes more wary. Flocks gather to bathe in ponds, eighty to ninety birds being the largest number recorded. (Colour photo: p. 120)

VOICE. Unique among Falkland birds in that it has no calls, but young in the nest make a strange hissing sound like a noisy intake of breath. This sound is rarely heard from full-grown birds.

FOOD. It takes carrion of all kinds and feeds from carcasses of sheep, cattle and birds. It also takes seals' faeces, and is disliked by sheep-farmers for its attacks on fallen sheep, from which they say it tears the eyes and tongue and may tear holes in the belly. There is much controversy over the question of whether the Turkey Vulture actually maims live sheep or waits till they are dead. It seems that the sheep must be badly weakened and unable to kick before this bird will attack them. Diddle-dee berries have been found in two birds' stomachs, but they may have come from the crops of goose carcasses.

HABITAT, STATUS & BREEDING. A common species which may be seen over both main and most of the outlying islands, although it is continually persecuted for its attacks on sheep. Darwin stated that this species was 'tolerably common' in 1833/34, and that it was one of 'only two carrion feeding hawks which have found their way to the Falkland Islands'. Now it is the most numerous bird of prey. It is particularly common at islands that support sea lion colonies, which probably provided its main food supply (excrement and dead seals) before the Islands were stocked by man. It has not only survived those periods when many seals were hunted (1790–1870, early 20th century and on a smaller scale 1928–40) but has increased its numbers. The increase in this species has occurred despite the price on its head for over sixty years, and it can probably be ascribed to the wool-based sheep-farming industry which annually provides many carcasses of culled sheep. An interesting fact is that on the few islands where the pugnacious Striated Caracara is numerous, the Turkey Vulture is absent or present in only very small numbers. It nests on tussock islands, sometimes in the mountains on the larger islands and rarely near settlements. The nest is simply a scrape on the ground beneath an overhanging tussock clump or rock, sometimes in caves or an old shanty. It lays 2 eggs, rarely 3, which are white with variable red-brown spots, blotches and lines. Eggs have been found in early September and late November, but most are laid between mid-September and late October. It often rears only one chick. Some juveniles are flying by mid-January but most do not fly till early February.

DISTRIBUTION ABROAD. The race *C. a. falklandica* is confined to the Falkland Is., but three other races inhabit South America from Tierra del Fuego through Chile and most of Argentina to Brazil and into Central America, the south-western United States and southern Canada.

Turkey Vulture awkwardly perched on a telegraph pole.

Red-backed Hawk

Buteo polyosoma (Quoy et Gaimard)   A. & C. Aguilucho común
Local names: Blue Hawk, Hawk

IDENTIFICATION. Male, medium, c19″. Female, medium-large, c21″. Wingspan: male c3′, female c4′. A large bird of prey, which is recognized in flight by its *broad 'fingered' wings, rounded head and short, square, black-tipped white tail. It glides with the wings almost flat, moving steadily forward* (cf. Turkey Vulture). It is very agile when hunting, and shoots low over ridges to surprise prey on the ground. It often hovers, with wings slightly flexed and the tail fanned, at heights between 20 and 200 ft. It is very aggressive when nesting and will swoop very close to an intruder, with talons extended. There are at least *two quite different colour phases* of both male and female as well as several immature plumages and a melanistic form. The tail of all adult males and females is always white with very narrow black bars and a subterminal black band. *Light Phase:* Male blue-grey above, darker on the wings; *white below.* Female has rich chestnut back and slaty-grey wings, also *white underparts. Dark Phase:* Male is *blue-grey above and below*, darker on the wings, but white on belly and under tail-coverts. Female is *dark red-brown below*, the back is rich chestnut and the wings slaty-grey above. The juvenile is generally dark brown streaked and flecked with buff above and below, *but the tail is grey closely barred with blackish.* Late during the second year of life the immature gradually acquires near-adult plumage of the light or dark type, and has the underparts more or less barred with red-brown. The adult has bright yellow legs and feet; in the immature bird they are duller. The claws are black, strongly hooked and very sharp. The bill is blue-grey with a black tip and is well hooked; the cere is yellow-green.

VOICE. It is generally silent outside the breeding season, although it sometimes calls when hunting. The call, which is most frequently heard from pairs near the nest, is a series of loud screams, 'keeeeow-kyow-kyow-kyow ...', higher-pitched in the male.

FOOD. It takes hares, rats, mice, rabbits and small birds, such as goslings and snipe. It also eats carrion and sometimes takes domestic fowls.

HABITAT, STATUS & BREEDING. Breeding sites are on high craggy peaks, but it may be seen over most parts of the Falkland Is. It is well distributed throughout the Falklands but not numerous. On East Falkland the nests are large structures of diddle-dee or fachine twigs; on West Falkland it uses 'box' twigs when available. Nests are built on cliff ledges and added to each year. It lays 2, occasionally 3, almost elliptical whitish eggs, variably marked with red-brown,

Female Red-backed Hawk; Tumbledown Mt.

Female Red-backed Hawk threatening to attack an intruder.

usually during October, but occasionally in late September.

DISTRIBUTION ABROAD. It is widely distributed in southern South America, being found in both mountainous and coastal regions of Central Colombia and Chile from 18°S to Tierra del Fuego. It also occurs in the Andean region of Argentina from about 20°S and on the Pampas from about 32°S to Tierra del Fuego. In winter it occurs throughout Argentina.

Striated Caracara

Phalcoboenus australis (Gmelin)   A. Caracara   C. Tiuque cordillerano austral
Local names: Johnny Rook, Jack Rook, King Jack Rook (adults)

IDENTIFICATION. Large. c24″. A large dark bird of prey, remarkable for its daring and *extreme tameness*, it resembles the Crested Caracara in shape and has similar but smaller white patches at the base of the primaries. It may be recognized in flight by its slightly smaller size, *all dark rounded head, shorter more rounded wings and black tail with a broad white terminal bar*. The adult male, and the female which is larger, have black plumage with white lanceolate flecks on nape, mantle, neck and breast and rufous tibia and lower belly. The cere and bare facial skin round the bill are orange; the bill is blue-white. The legs and feet are orange-yellow. In juvenile and first year plumage it is dark brown including the tibia and belly, *speckled with rufous-buff on nape, mantle and breast*; the tail is lighter brown and buffish towards the tip; the bill is slate-grey with yellowish facial skin and the legs and feet are probably also slaty. A second year bird has buff wing patches and retains the rufous speckling on the mantle and breast; the tail is dark brown with a buff terminal band; the bill is whitish, the facial skin yellow and the legs and feet dull yellow. The *crop*, which has *orange-yellow skin*, protrudes prominently from the neck feathers when it is full. It is very inquisitive and mischievous, having also a peculiar addiction for bright articles such as knives, which it will steal within a few feet of a man. It can run fast and its flight is much more agile than the Crested Caracara's. (Colour photo: p. 153)

voice. It is a noisy bird and has several calls, one of which is a 'caw' very

Two first-year Striated Caracaras on West Point Island.

like that of the European Rook (*Corvus frugilegus*), from which the 18th century sealers derived its local name. Another common call is a loud wailing scream, uttered with the head thrown up and backwards.

FOOD. It eats all kinds of carrion as well as taking goslings, young penguins and other young birds. Two or three together are reputed to be able to catch and kill an adult Upland Goose between them, by sidling up to it from both sides and using their strong legs and feet to hold the goose's foot to the ground while attacking it. It is also said to kill lambs and to take the eyes and tongues from fallen sheep, but there is still much controversy in the Falkland Is. over the amount of harm this bird does to sheep.

HABITAT, STATUS & BREEDING. Until the 1830s at least this bird was, in Charles Darwin's words, 'exceedingly numerous at the Falkland Is.', and was 'extraordinarily tame and fearless and constantly haunted the neighbourhood of houses to pick up all kinds of offal'. Cobb (1910) reported that it had 'decreased in numbers in the Falkland Islands of late years'. It is now confined to the extreme west of West Falkland and outlying islands such as Grand and Steeple Jason, the Passage Is., Elephant Cays and Beauchêne I. where it is still common. Visiting birds are also seen at West Point I. and other places on West Falkland. The great reduction in its numbers is due to its peculiar tameness and the fact that many sheep-farmers consider it a danger to the sheep. Since the 1920s it has been officially protected, but it is still shot on some islands. It nests on cliffs, building the nest of tussock-grass or diddle-dee twigs and lining it with grass and wool. It lays 2–3 dark reddish-spotted cream eggs in October or November.

DISTRIBUTION ABROAD. It has a very restricted range, being found only on islands south of the Beagle Channel, Staten I., and on the southeast and southern coasts of Tierra del Fuego.

Crested Caracara

Polyborus plancus (Miller)   A. Carancho   C. Traro
Local name: Carancho

IDENTIFICATION. Medium-large to large. c22–25″. This large dark brown bird of prey is easily recognized in flight by its *long, broad 'fingered' wings with large white primary patches*, showing little or no backward curve and appearing the same width throughout; *long, square, whitish tail with a broad terminal black bar, and the heavy black cap on the head*. The flying action consists of short butterfly-like

Crested Caracara; immature bird landing.

flaps interspersed with glides when the wings are held flat or slightly down-bent. The adult is dark brown above and below with fine buff barring on back and breast, and uniform dark brown on the belly and its feathered tibia. Ear-coverts, nape, throat and neck are sandy-buff while the forehead and crown to the eye are jet-black, with *elongated crown feathers forming a ragged crest* above the nape. This cap, which contrasts sharply with the buff face and neck, gives it *a flat-headed appearance, noticeable from long distances when the bird is perched.* Its very deep, strongly hooked bill is greenish-white, while the cere and bare skin between bill and eye are orange with short black bristles. The long legs are yellow. Immature birds have more dark brown on neck and breast, which with the back are heavily streaked with buff. The bill is pale blue-grey or yellowish and the facial skin varies between dull crimson and pale pink. It walks and runs well on its long legs. Although usually rather shy, flocks of young birds in winter are inquisitive and will approach within 30 yds. of a stationary observer. During the breeding season it is often mobbed in flight by South American Terns, Black Oystercatchers and sometimes by Dolphin Gulls. It has even been mobbed when perched, by Skuas and Terns. It is seen singly or in pairs and in winter sometimes as many as twenty-five, mostly young birds, gather in flocks.

VOICE. The usual call is a very harsh loud 'cruk', uttered singly or repeated quickly in a higher pitch. When a bird is perched this call is sometimes given five or more times in rapid succession, suddenly followed by a loud, purring call uttered with the head laid back on the shoulders and then followed by more 'cruk' calls as the head returns to a normal position.

FOOD. It eats carrion of many kinds, including dead penguins, sheep and cattle. One was seen eating a dead octopus on a beach in Stanley harbour, and beetle elytra have been found in pellets. It also attacks fallen sheep, for which it is regarded as a pest and has a price on its beak. Some farmers consider that a 'Carancho' attacking a newly-fallen sheep will give it the stimulus to stagger to its feet, thus saving a sheep which survives where shepherds are scarce. Food is carried, when necessary, in the feet. A resting ledge near a nest on Kidney I. had the remains (three legs) of a hare on it, in December 1960. This carcass or part of it, must have been carried at least half a mile in flight from the nearest part of the mainland.

HABITAT, STATUS & BREEDING. Darwin did not report this species from the Falklands in 1833/34, but it is widespread now presumably because it can rely on the sheep-farming industry to supply some of its food requirements. Although it may seen almost anywhere over the islands, it is only locally common, particularly amongst the crags and higher outcrops. The nest is a large structure of diddle-dee twigs, bones and grass, lined with wool, which is added to each year. It is placed on a rock ledge in the mountains or on a coastal cliff and is usually inaccessible. It lays 2, sometimes 3 eggs, which vary from cream blotched with dark red to deep brownish-red. They are laid in the period between mid-September and October, but one nest was found with a single egg in late August 1961 near Rincon Grande.

DISTRIBUTION ABROAD. This race, *P. p. plancus*, is found throughout Argentina and Chile, also in Paraguay and Uruguay. It is much more abundant in the southern half of Chile from 37°S to Tierra del Fuego than it is in the north. Another race is found from the Guianas, Venezuela and Colombia to north-western Peru and Amazonia.

Peregrine Falcon

Falco peregrinus cassini Sharpe
A. Halcón viajero   C. Halcón peregrino austral
Local names: Sparrow Hawk, Black Hawk

IDENTIFICATION. Male, small-medium, c15″. Female, medium, c19″. This medium size bird of prey is easily recognized by its characteristic dashing flight, typical outline, and very dark head and upper surface. *Its wings are long, strongly curved and taper sharply to a point*; the tail is long and tapered. *It is very dark slate-grey above with a sooty-brown head and prominent dark 'moustaches'*, and heavily barred brown and buff breast and undersides of the wings. The flight is powerful and fast, with rapid shallow beats and occasional straight glides with the wings held almost horizontal. The usual mode of hunting is to stoop at great speed on flying birds and strike them with the talons as it passes. It also commonly chases birds in straight flight and can hover for a few seconds even in a 30 knot wind. When perched the *sooty-brown head and 'moustaches'* are very noticeable; it also shows the reddish-buff neck lightly streaked with dark brown, and breast and flanks whitish heavily barred with dark brown. The female is darker than the male but the extent of barring on the underparts varies considerably in both sexes. The legs and feet are yellow, the cere green-yellow and the bill is blue-grey. The juvenile is darker than the adult and has heavily streaked neck and breast, not barred. The bill and cere are both blue-grey, while the legs and feet vary from blue-grey to green-yellow.

VOICE. The usual flight call is a short sharp 'kek', sometimes repeated quickly. It has various other high-pitched chattering and squeaky notes used mainly when breeding.

FOOD. Mainly birds taken in flight, ranging in size from House Sparrow and Tussock-bird to Upland Goose. It has been seen chasing Falkland Thrush and Long-tailed Meadowlark in flight, but was foiled each time by the intended victim gaining shelter. It occasionally takes domestic fowls or one of the few domestic pigeons. It commonly kills prions; one was flushed from a prion's remains near the south shore of Stanley Common on 27th July 1958. This prion must have been near the Falkland coast at a date when it is thought to be pelagic in the South Atlantic.

HABITAT, STATUS & BREEDING. It may be observed almost anywhere over the Falkland Is., but is not numerous. Breeding sites are on cliffs, usually coastal but sometimes on inland crags. More pairs breed on islands off West Falkland where large colonies of prions are found. It lays 3, sometimes 2 or 4, heavily marked red-brown eggs on an inaccessible ledge with few nest materials, between late September and late October. It has been shot, more in the past than now, for its attacks on domestic fowls.

DISTRIBUTION ABROAD. This race, *F. p. cassini* inhabits southern South America from Tierra del Fuego to 28°S in Chile and to about 42°S in Argentina. Several other races occur in most parts of the world.

American Kestrel

Falco sparverius cinnamominus Swainson
A. Halconcito común   C. Cernícalo común

IDENTIFICATION. Small. c11". A small falcon, about Thrush size, with long tail and sharply pointed wings. The male has a *blue-grey head*, white cheeks, black 'moustache' stripes and a black half-collar round the hind neck. The *back is rich chestnut* lightly barred with black; wing-coverts and secondaries blue-grey spotted with black; primaries mainly black; *tail chestnut with a broad black sub-terminal bar* and white tip. Underparts are mainly creamy with dark brown spots on the flanks. The female is slightly larger and has a similar head pattern to the male, but *all the back and wing-coverts are red-brown thickly barred with black*. The *tail is chestnut with many black bars*, the underparts creamy, well streaked with brown. Cere and legs are yellow and the bill is bluish. Juvenile resembles the female. When hunting it hovers to sight small animals and insects on the ground.

140

HABITAT, STATUS & RECORDS. May possibly breed in the northeast corner of West Falkland. It haunts many different types of country in South America and frequently nests in holes in cliffs, which is probably the only suitable nest-site available in the Falkland Is. Three specimens were collected in the 19th century and are now in the British Museum. A female was obtained in 1930 by J. E. Hamilton, who also collected a male on 24th September 1945 which had been caught in a pole-trap at Cape Orford; a male died on West Point I. in March 1954; these three skins are also in the British Museum. One was shot in 1909 and another was seen around Stanley during most of 1924 (A. G. Bennett). A single bird was seen east of Stanley on 5th August 1951 and the most recent record is of one caught and later released at Black Shanty, near Fox Bay in 1955. All these records appear to be of solitary vagrants which survived for varying periods, rather than residents. No adults with juveniles have ever been seen, so far as is known.

DISTRIBUTION ABROAD. The race *F. s. cinnamominus* is found in Bolivia, Brazil, Paraguay, Uruguay, Argentina and most of Chile to Tierra del Fuego. Other races are found in Central and North America.

Red-gartered Coot

Fulica armillata Vieillot   A. Gallareta pico rojo   C. Tagua común

IDENTIFICATION. Medium. 16–18″. *All black plumage, short neck, rounded 'tail-less' body and jerky movements of the small head when swimming* distinguish a Coot from any ducks with which it may associate on ponds. This species and two others, the Red-fronted (*F. rufifrons*), and White-winged (*F. leucoptera*) (*see* Vagrants list) are all similarly coloured, but can be separated by the colour of the bill and frontal shield. They all have velvet-black heads and necks, and grey-black body plumage. Their long legs and feet with broadly lobed toes are set far back on the body. The colour of the feet varies from dark olive to paler yellow-green. The Red-gartered has a *bright red 'garter'* just above the ankle joint. *Red-gartered is largest;* has a stout greenish-yellow bill with blood-red culmen and a red spot at the base of each mandible. Frontal shield is *oval, yellow bordered with red.* Red-fronted is *intermediate* in size (small-medium, c14″); has lemon-yellow bill with red base to each mandible; *all red* lengthened and *pointed frontal shield reaches to the top of the forehead.* White-winged is *smallest* (small-medium, 12–13″); has whole bill and *projecting* frontal shield lemon-yellow *lacking any red.* The wings are comparatively short and their flight appears weak with rapid wing-beats. On taking flight they patter over the water for some yards before becoming airborne.

HABITAT, STATUS & RECORDS. All three species frequent ponds, lakes and rivers in South America; in the Falkland Is. occasional vagrants may be seen on fair-sized ponds or lakes. Several Red-gartered Coots have been seen or shot since the first was caught near Stanley on 23rd May 1923. All records are of single birds, except three seen together at Calm Head, Port Stephens early in 1951; one of these was shot and subsequently identified. An immature male shot on a weed-grown pond near Stanley on 14th December 1960 is the most recent record.

DISTRIBUTION ABROAD. Numerous in southern South America from 23°S in Brazil and 30°S in Chile through Paraguay, Uruguay and Argentina to Tierra del Fuego, but replaced in the high Andes by the White-winged Coot.

Magellanic Oystercatcher

Haematopus leucopodus Garnot   A. Ostrero del Sur   C. Pilpilén austral
Local names: Black-and-white Curlew, Pied Oystercatcher

IDENTIFICATION. Medium. c17″. A familiar bird of the sandy beaches, it is easily recognized by the combination of *conspicuously pied plumage, long bright orange-red bill* and fairly large size. In flight it shows *a distinctive triangular white secondary patch* on its black wings and *a broad black distal half to the white tail*. The head, breast and back are shiny blue-black; the rest of the underparts are white. It has stout, flesh-pink legs and pink feet, a striking orange iris and yellow orbital ring. The immature is similarly patterned but has buff flecks on the black plumage and a dull orange bill with a black tip. The flight is strong with quick shallow wing-beats and *its flight-note is diagnostic*. Flocks up to a hundred are seen from January to August, sometimes with Black Oystercatchers. It is very antagonistic towards other birds and man when it has young or eggs, although its first reaction to a man approaching the nest is to draw him away by injury-feigning. It will attack birds from the Sanderling to the Skua and Turkey Vulture in size. (Colour photo: p. 153)

VOICE. The most frequent call, which is the flight-note and is also heard from flocks on the beach, is a loud long-drawn plaintive whistle, 'peeee', often wavering and rising in tone towards the end. When a flock calls together a peculiar discordant sound is made as some birds use slightly higher notes than others. When it is excited it utters a higher-pitched rapid 'pee-pee-pee-pee . . .'.

142

Pair of Magellanic Oystercatchers displaying; near the Round Pond, Stanley Common.

In displays, when one or both of a pair walk or run with the bill lowered till it touches the ground and the tail raised high and fanned, a loud sharp 'keep' is used, often repeated. Another high squeaky call is also heard in displays. It can often be heard calling at night.

FOOD. The main items of its diet are 'sand-worms' up to 1 ft. long which it extracts from beaches, and limpets and mussels which are prised from rocks at low tide. It also eats lice from under beach rocks which it tips up, and will eat jelly-fish which are often stranded on the beaches. Three birds were watched feeding on limpets at Eliza Cove on 14th October 1961. The limpets were on a rocky beach and the tide was low, although the birds often took limpets in 3 in. of water. Their method of removal involved probing at the edge of the shell where it was attached, then delivering rapid woodpecker-like hammer blows to break a section of shell from the edge about $\frac{1}{2}$ to $\frac{3}{4}$ in. long and $\frac{1}{4}$ in. deep. The bill was then inserted by laying the head sideways and the limpet levered off by lifting the head. The largest specimen removed was $2\frac{1}{4} \times 1\frac{1}{2}$ in. with a $\frac{1}{2} \times \frac{1}{4}$ in. section removed.

HABITAT, STATUS & BREEDING. A common and widely spread species, it is apparently more numerous than the Black Oystercatcher, but this impression may be due to its habit of flocking in winter and to its conspicuous colouring. It is mainly a bird of the sand beaches and shallow rock beaches with mussel beds. Freshwater ponds are visited by flocks in winter apparently for roosting. The nest is merely a scrape in sand or a depression in the soil, which sometimes contains small pebbles, pieces of dry kelp or dry sheep droppings. It may be partly sheltered amongst diddle-dee or dead kelp but is often exposed. The majority of nests are found at the top of beaches above high water mark, although some are 50 yds. from the beach on short turf or in short tussock-grass. 2 olive-brown or greenish eggs marked with black are laid. They are darker than the Black Oystercatcher's eggs. The main laying season is from the last week of September to middle or late October, but eggs have been found in the second week of September, during November and as late as mid-December.

DISTRIBUTION ABROAD. The species *H. leucopodus* is a common bird in the Magellanic region of South America. It is found throughout the many islands on the Pacific coast from Cape Horn to 42°S in Chile and occasionally reaches 40°S. On the Atlantic side it ranges from Staten I., through Tierra del Fuego and is found both inland and on the coast of Argentina to about 43°S.

Black Oystercatcher

Haematopus ater Vieillot et Oudart   A. Ostrero negro   C. Pilpilén negro
Local name: Black Curlew

IDENTIFICATION. Medium-large. c20″. This shorebird is unmistakable with its *completely blackish plumage, deep and long, bright scarlet bill* and incongruous thick flesh-pink legs and feet. Its head, neck and underparts are slaty-black while the back and upper surface of the wings are very dark brown. The prominent iris is yellow with a bright red eye-ring. The juvenile and immature resemble the adult, but are flecked with buff until about one year old, have grey legs at first and blackish bills streaked with orange. It is a quiet bird (except when breeding) and often escapes notice on a rocky beach or among dead kelp, only the red bill revealing its presence when it moves. In flight its silhouette of a long deep bill, all dark plumage and long wings with quick wing-beats easily identifies it. *The loud often-used flight-note is also diagnostic.* It is usually seen in pairs or small parties, although some associate with Magellanic Oystercatchers in winter flocks. The largest party recorded consisted of three adults and five first year birds in late

Black Oystercatcher defending its nest.

July 1959. It is often active at dusk and may be heard calling till well after dark. On Kidney I. during the breeding season, the only birds towards which antagonistic behaviour was shown were 'Caranchos', and they were sometimes chased hard and high in the air for up to half a minute. When a man approaches a nest with eggs, the adults both walk quietly away at first, but if he stops by the nest one bird starts calling and may fly close by his head. It may also attempt to lead him away by injury-feigning. When with young, both parents call loudly.

VOICE. The flight-note is a loud clear 'keep' or 'keeup', with an abrupt ending, quite different from the Magellanic species' call. When excited and in display it utters a very rapid vibratory whistle or slow trill, which rises in speed and pitch, then slows and falls as it dies away. It may be heard in flight or from pairs displaying on the ground. Pairs have been seen displaying together in late March and early April. One pair near Darwin on 24th March 1958 faced each other 2 ft. apart, bowed till their bills almost touched the ground then lifted their heads quickly. The performance lasted about 30 seconds and was accompanied throughout by the shrill vibratory whistle from both birds. A pair in flight at Kidney I. on 9th April 1961 called frequently while one bird flew with peculiar slow wing-beats, then glided short distances with the wings held up at about a 45° angle and the head bent down. One bird was calling vibratory whistling notes.

FOOD. Limpets and mussels form the main part of the diet. Limpets are removed from rocks by a sharp jab of the bill and a quick levering movement of bill and head, without breaking the shell. (This species has a stronger bill than the Magellanic; *see* under FOOD of that species.) Mussels are wedged into rock crevices before being opened. Around three nest-sites on Kidney I. (all on rocky ridges and one of them on an isolated rock outlier about 35 ft. above the sea) were scattered empty shells of mussels and limpets mostly 1 to 1½ in., but some 3 in. in diameter. These were obviously carried up to feed the chicks which stay close by their nests until fledged. One nest had about a hundred limpet and mussel shells, lodged in hollows, within a radius of a few feet.

HABITAT, STATUS & BREEDING. This species is well distributed round all coasts of the Falkland Is., although it is possibly more common on the east side of East Falkland. It is thought to be less numerous than the Magellanic species. It lives almost exclusively on rocky beaches, although single birds are occasionally seen resting on sand beaches. It also frequents shallow tidal beaches where mussels abound. Small parties are seen in sheltered creeks during the winter, most of them being immature birds. Pairs appear to remain in or near their breeding territories through the winter. The breeding season starts later than the Magellanic's. 2, sometimes only 1, grey-buff or buff eggs spotted and streaked below and on the surface with yellow-brown and purple-brown, are laid during November. A few are laid at the end of October while fresh eggs have been found as late as 27th January. These January clutches are probably replacements for earlier lost clutches. The nest is a scrape on sand or a sheltered corner among beach rocks often containing a few small pebbles, small mussel shells and fragments of dead kelp. The nest is usually within a few yards of the shore, but one at the Lagoon near Bluff Cove, in January 1960 and 1961 was on a long shingle bank, over 100 yds. from the sandy shore and close to a large Kelp Gull colony.

DISTRIBUTION ABROAD. *H. ater* has an exceptionally wide latitudinal distribution being resident on the west coast of South America from Cape Horn and the Magellanic islands along the whole Chilean coast to 7°S on the Peruvian coast. It is also resident on the Argentine coast from Staten I. to about 43°S. In winter, occurs as far north as the mouth of the River Plate (35°S).

Southern Lapwing

Vanellus chilensis (Molina)   A. Tero-tero   C. Queltegüe común
Local name: Teru

IDENTIFICATION. Small-medium. 14–15″. A large plover, *strikingly patterned black, white and grey*, with a characteristic penetrating cry. The female is slightly larger than the male. Plumage generally grey above with a bronzy patch on the scapulars; rounded head and neck grey but for black on the forehead and round the bill linked by a thin line with the extensive black area of the breast. Remainder of underparts white, including under wing-coverts. Upper tail-coverts white. Tail white with terminal half black tipped with white. A wispy black crest falls from the nape. Bill slender, red with a black tip. Legs quite long, dark crimson. Iris crimson. Each wing has a sharp ½-in. spur at the carpal joint, which is sometimes visible in flight. Flies with slow beats of its *broad rounded wings showing grey back, white wing centre and black tips, and white and black tail*. Wary and noisy, it calls loudly whenever it is flushed uttering a harsh, rather nasal 'parp-peup-peup-peup'. Runs quickly and feeds by tilting the whole body forward to pick from the ground.

HABITAT, STATUS & RECORDS. A bird of the fertile pastures in Argentina and Chile, it is most likely to be seen in the Falkland Is. around settlements and the better grazing near water. Occurs fairly often, on an average less than once a year and usually singly, but there are two records of three together; at San Carlos and Walker Creek in 1953. Dated records are in March 1913 and 1924, September–October 1961 (2) and 1962. Vagrants in the Falkland Is. are probably drifted from the southern breeding population of Tierra del Fuego and southern Argentina by strong westerly winds in the spring and autumn migration periods.

DISTRIBUTION ABROAD. A common species throughout most of Argentina and Chile from about 25°S to Tierra del Fuego. It also occurs in the Guianas, Venezuela, Colombia, Brazil, Bolivia, Paraguay and Uruguay. The population of southern Argentina and southern Chile from Tierra del Fuego to about 45°S has been described as a separate race, *V. c. fretensis*, which is almost identical to *V. c. chilensis*, but smaller.

Two-banded Plover

Charadrius falklandicus Latham
A. Chorlo doble collar   C. Chorlo de doble collar
Local names: Plover, Two-barred Plover

IDENTIFICATION. Very small. c7″. A small, plump and active *black, white and grey-brown bird* that is typical of Falkland sand beaches, it is usually quite tame and often prefers to run rather than fly when disturbed. The adult male is light grey-brown above, has pure white forehead, lores and underparts, *a broad black crescent on the breast and a narrow black bar across the neck*. A black bar crosses the crown through the eyes and joins each end of the neck bar. *The rest of the head is bright chestnut*. The adult female resembles the male but has a mainly brown nape; the black breast bands are also less extensive. In late summer and autumn both male and female are duller. The juvenile is brown flecked with buff on the back, wing-coverts and head, with a short buff eye-stripe, and variable, often incomplete dark brown breast and neck bands. It attains adult plumage in the following summer. The short bill and legs are black. In flight it shows a faint white bar on the primaries and a dark tail with white sides. Flocks of young and old birds gather at sand beaches from mid-December onwards, reaching maximum numbers in January (up to 150 recorded at Surf Bay). Flocks of fifty or more can easily be overlooked, as when they are not feeding they sit quietly amongst pebbles and boulders above sand beaches, or in the lee of dead kelp and sand hummocks just above high water mark. (Colour photo: p. 153)

VOICE. The most frequent call-notes are a liquid 'prink' or 'prit' used as a flight-note, and a thin squeaky 'tseet' used when running. A low harsh 'chut' and an explosive tittering 'prrrrit' are uttered mostly by males chasing each other within flocks. In the injury-feigning display commonly given by the female, though sometimes by the male, a very low buzzing note is uttered while the bird creeps away with wings spread and bent forward and the tail fanned and depressed. This display is given when there are eggs or young nearby.

FOOD. It feeds mainly on small insects and worms which it picks from the surf edge, from heaps of rotted kelp or from areas of short grass and sand. It also commonly feeds and bathes round pools of fresh water behind beaches, at mussel beds covered with seaweed and at rock pools.

HABITAT, STATUS & BREEDING. It is a locally common resident being found round the coasts and islands where there are sand beaches and muddy creeks, and is often seen with White-rumped Sandpipers during the summer. Between September and December it is also found on dry slopes of short grass and diddle-dee, often up to a mile from the sea. Nesting starts in late September and eggs may be found from then to mid-January, although later clutches after November are probably replacements. There is no evidence that it rears more than one brood. The nest is a scrape, often on a small hummock, amongst short grass, diddle-dee or ferns, or may be on a beach amongst dead dry kelp. It is some-times lined with a few wisps of grass. It lays 2–3, occasionally 4, greenish or buff eggs, blotched and spotted with dark and light brown, mainly at the larger end.

Between October 1957 and December 1959 twenty-eight were trapped by clap-net, then banded and colour-banded at Surf Bay, Rookery Bay and Yorke Point, $3\frac{1}{2}$ miles east, and at Lake Point Bay, $2\frac{1}{2}$ miles south of Stanley. One juvenile banded at Lake Point Bay on 29th March 1959, was seen there the following December in adult female plumage and watched injury-feigning. It was seen at the same place twice more in September 1960. These recoveries and sight-recoveries of others indicate a close attachment to one area; the longest movement recorded is $1\frac{1}{2}$ miles from Yorke Point to Surf Bay on the other side of Cape Pembroke peninsula (three of nine banded). An adult male banded near Rookery Bay in November 1958 and retrapped once, was seen twelve times during the following twenty-three months, three times where banded and nine times within a mile at Surf Bay and the Canache. From examination of trapped birds it is apparent that moult and replacement of the flight feathers are effected over a long period, although the actual dates vary considerably between individuals. Some adults probably start losing the inner primaries early in December and have replaced them all by early March, while others still have old second and third (outer) primaries at the same date. One examined on 3rd April had all new primaries, but the two outer long primaries were not fully extended.

DISTRIBUTION ABROAD. The species *Ch. falklandicus* is a common summer visitor to southern South America, breeding from Tierra del Fuego and the Magellanic islands to about 50°S in Argentina and Chile. Much smaller num-bers breed further north in Argentina and Chile to about 24°S. It migrates north in winter and occurs in southeastern Brazil, Uruguay and northern Chile.

Rufous-chested Dotterel

Zonibyx modestus (Lichtenstein)   A. Chorlo pecho colorado   C. Chorlo negro
Local name: Dotterel

IDENTIFICATION. Small. 8–9″. This beautiful long-legged plover is unmistakable in breeding plumage (mid-August to December). The adult has *a broad white head stripe extending from above and behind the eye round the forehead.* The face and throat are blue-grey while *the breast is bright chestnut with a broad, black band separating it from the white belly*, which has an orange streak behind the leg. Crown, nape and upperparts are dark brown. The sharp-pointed bill is black and the legs are grey-green. The female is slightly duller than the male. A juvenile is recognized by the scaly pattern of dark brown heavily streaked and spotted with buff on the back; its whole breast is brown and it has no white head stripe. Downy chicks are golden-buff blotched with black above, and have a distinctive cinnamon patch on the hind neck which immediately separates them from Two-banded Plover chicks. By mid-December the adult begins to lose the chestnut and black breast, grey face and white stripe, and by the end of March has assumed winter plumage, which consists of a buff head stripe and all brown neck and breast. Some birds retain traces of the black band through the winter. It has a very rapid flight, shows broad white sides to its blackish tail and white shaft streaks on the outer primaries; the white head stripe is also prominent in flight. When nesting it is always alert and active, one of the pair often standing on guard on a small mound uttering its distinctive plaintive call at intervals. (Colour photo: p. 154)

VOICE. The most frequent call, uttered whenever it is flushed, is a loud whistle, 'p*eeoo*', often with a peculiar tremulous quality. It has several variations on this call, including a rapid repetition and a longer-drawn version used by adults standing guard when nesting. During courtship when the male (probably) flies with an unusual slow-motion wing action and glides with wings raised, up to a 100 ft. above its territory, it utters a low regular 'tik-tik-tik' alternating with a loud whirring or rattling call. It also utters a loud wheezy 'wh*ea*r' followed by the rattling call in sexual flight when the male pursues the female, or both chase off other Rufous-chested Dotterels. Parents show anxiety by calling when their young are disturbed, but have no injury-feigning display.

FOOD. Insects of many kinds, including burrowing larvae.

HABITAT, STATUS & BREEDING. A common species, it occurs in a wide variety of habitats from mussel beds, boulder or sand beaches and mudflats, to flooded grassland, eroded slopes and Hard Camp. It often associates with Two-banded Plover on mudflats, particularly during the spring (August–September) and autumn (February–March). Between January and March flocks up to at least a hundred strong gathered on bare, eroded ridges of clay and loose rocks near Yorke Bay. These appeared to be pre-migration gatherings, but it is not yet certain what proportion of the population does leave the Falklands. Some are seen from April to July, usually in small parties on grassland near the coast. Abbott (1861) stated that it entirely disappeared by the end of April. Bennett (1926) and Cawkell & Hamilton (1961) stated that although most migrated, a few remained through the winter. There are records of flocks mounting high in the air and moving off westward or northwest from Stanley Common and from West Point I. Pettingill (1960) considers it unlikely that this species regularly leaves the Falklands in autumn against the prevailing winds. The plumage from March to early August is very dull and parties of birds behave quietly. This is in marked contrast to their courtship-flying and loud calling when the species suddenly becomes conspicuous late in August and through September. It is likely that more are present in winter than has been thought and that they are not noticed. When breeding it resorts to drier slopes of the open country, particularly where diddle-dee and fern are abundant. It nests between late September and mid-January, although the main laying period is in October. Later clutches are probably replacements. 2 eggs only are laid, of an olive-brown colour heavily blotched with black, but reddish eggs are sometimes found. The nest is merely a scrape sheltered by ferns, diddle-dee or white grass clumps.

DISTRIBUTION ABROAD. This species is a common breeding bird in Tierra del Fuego and the Magellanic islands. It also breeds less commonly on the Chilean coast and islands to about 42°S. Most migrate north in winter and it is then found on low ground between about 40° and 27°S in Argentina, Chile and Uruguay, occasionally to 23°S in eastern Brazil. Some remain in the Beagle Channel area south of Tierra del Fuego during the winter.

White-rumped Sandpiper

Calidris fuscicollis (Vieillot)
A. Chorlito rabadilla blanca   C. Playero de lomo blanco

IDENTIFICATION. Very small. c6¾″. A very small, slender, shore bird; in winter plumage as it is usually seen in the Falkland Is., it is grey-brown on head and back with dark streaking and mainly white below but streaked with brown on the breast. It is inconspicuous on the ground and can be confused with the juvenile Two-banded Plover, but *on flying frequently calls a diagnostic squeaky 'jeet'*, shows *a white patch above the dark tail* and a thin white wing-bar. When seen in the company of Two-banded Plovers its longer, more slender black bill also helps to identify it. Moult into breeding plumage commences in March; the back and crown feathers then show variable buff margins; the white underparts become more clearly streaked with dark brown on the breast and have larger streaks down the sides of the body to the flanks. (Colour photo: p. 154)

HABITAT, STATUS & RECORDS. A common non-breeding visitor to the Falkland Is. from arctic North America, it is often found with Two-banded Plover on the sandy shores of creeks, on flat sand beaches with pools of water where stranded dead kelp gives shelter, and at the grassy margins of freshwater pools near sand beaches. It also forages on tidal mudflats, sand spits where mussels abound, and boulder beaches with freshly stranded kelp; it is less frequently seen on marshy grassland away from the seashore and occasionally at the surf edge of ocean beaches. Occurs in small parties and flocks sometimes up to seventy strong and occasionally much larger. Maximum recorded is c350 at Bertha's Beach, Island Harbour, East Falkland on 20th January 1963. Migrants arrive during September and October (earliest record, three at Lake Point Bay, south of Stanley on 12th September 1960) and large numbers are present until they leave again in March and April (latest records, eighteen on 20th March 1961; about seven on 27th March 1962; two on 19th April 1959, all at Surf Bay).

DISTRIBUTION ABROAD. Breeds on the arctic coasts of North America and migrates south through the West Indies to winter in South America east of the Andes from Paraguay, Uruguay, southern Brazil and Argentina to the Magellanic region and Tierra del Fuego. Occasionally recorded in Chile as far north as 25°S.

Sanderling

Calidris alba (Pallas)   A. Chorlito blanco   C. Playero común

IDENTIFICATION. Small. c8″. A plump little wader, about the size of a Two-banded Plover, *but more heavily built* and with a *longer black bill*. It is easily recognized in winter plumage by its *white face and underparts, pale grey back*, blackish shoulder patch and edge to the wing. In flight it can be immediately separated from both the White-rumped Sandpiper and Two-banded Plover by a *long, broad white bar on the blackish wings*, dark tail with white sides and white underparts. It is extremely active and often feeds along the surf edge, scampering over

ABOVE Adult Striated Caracara on cliff-edge at West Point I. (*see p.* 134).
BELOW LEFT Magellanic Oystercatchers flying at Bertha's Beach (*see p.* 142).
BELOW RIGHT Adult male Two-banded Plover at Watt Cove, East Falkland
(*see p.* 148).

the sands after the receding waves. The call-note closely resembles that of the Two-banded Plover.

HABITAT, STATUS & RECORDS. It has been recorded only on or near extensive sand beaches in the Falkland Is. on seven occasions since the first in November 1937 at Cape Dolphin; the earliest date is 23rd September 1958 and the latest 22nd March 1945, both at Surf Bay. Four more records of between one and four birds were made at Surf Bay and Yorke Bay, east of Stanley in February and September 1958, January and March 1959. About seventy were present at Bertha's Beach, East Falkland on 19/20th January 1963 with the largest gathering of White-rumped Sandpiper (c350) recorded in the Falkland Is. Prior to these recent records, the Sanderling was considered to be only an accidental visitor from its regular wintering areas on the coasts of Argentina and Chile. The presence of seventy at one of the largest and most rarely scrutinized sand beaches in the Falkland Is. probably indicates that it is a regular wintering visitor, although in much smaller numbers than the White-rumped Sandpiper.

DISTRIBUTION ABROAD. Breeds on arctic islands of Canada and northern Greenland, also at Spitsbergen and in Siberia. North American birds migrate through North and South America to winter from the southern U.S.A. to 47°S in Chile and in Argentina as far south as Tierra del Fuego.

Common Snipe

Gallinago gallinago (Vieillot)   A. & C. Becasina común
Local name: Snipe

IDENTIFICATION. Small. c10". A small ground-loving bird with *a very long 2–2½ in. bill, it appears generally sandy-buff with dark markings* as it runs between the grasses and diddle-dee. The brown head with a large dark eye, has *broad longitudinal black and buff stripes from bill to nape*. The back and wings are black spangled and streaked with chestnut and buff, with *a long broad buff line down the scapulars* and a shorter line on the median coverts. The underparts are white, heavily mottled with dark brown on neck, breast and flanks. The bill is light brown with a dark tip and the long legs are yellow-green. The juvenile resembles the adult but has a dark bill and blue-grey legs at first. This species is unusually tame and much prefers to run when disturbed. When flushed it flies erratically for 10–15 yds. before pitching.

VOICE. When flushed it utters a short harsh 'skerp'. From early August to October, less often to mid-January and occasionally in June, it performs in a

ABOVE LEFT Adult Rufous-chested Dotterel on Hard Camp (*see p.* 150).   155
ABOVE RIGHT White-rumped Sandpiper on Surf Bay, East Falkland (*see p.* 151).
BELOW Party of Sanderling at Bertha's Beach (*see p.* 152).

Common Snipe wading in a pond near Stanley.

nocturnal display-flight, circling high in the air and producing a musical bleating sound with the spread rigid outer tail feathers. This 'drumming' is heard for about two hours after dusk, again for an hour before dawn, and has occasionally been heard in mid-afternoon. At the same season a loud 'chippa-chippa-chippa' call is also heard after dusk. When adults have small young, they utter a peculiar ventriloquial 'tik-tok-tik-tok', like a large clock ticking slowly, which carries a long way. Another call is a quieter low 'tip-tip-tip'. An adult anxious about its young utters 'tik-tok' notes more rapidly and displays with wings slightly dropped and tail held vertical, fanned and twisted sideways through almost 90°; it also utters a wailing 'wow' when anxious. The young have a weak 'see-see-see' call.

156

FOOD. It has been observed digging for earthworms, which are probably its staple diet.

HABITAT, STATUS & BREEDING. A fairly common species, widely distributed in the Falkland Is., it was far more numerous many years ago when hundreds were shot each autumn at Lively I. It apparently used to gather there before migration (C. & H. 1961). It may have become less common through a combination of excessive shooting and grass-burning in the nesting season. It is found on wet parts of the open country, where there is rank growth of white grass or rushes. but it is also seen on dry ground with diddle-dee cover and on George I. feeds at rotted kelp heaps on beaches. It has been noted about 1,000 ft. above sea level on West Point I. on a dry eroded peat slope amongst planted tussock- and sand grass. Although it is thought to migrate in autumn some are present in winter, but they rarely call and are inconspicuous. It lays 2, rarely 3, pear-shaped olive-green eggs, spotted and blotched with black, in a slight grass-lined nest amongst grasses or low diddle-dee clumps. Eggs or young have been found in all months between July and February, but the main laying season is probably August to September.

DISTRIBUTION ABROAD. This species, represented by four races, inhabits most of South America from Cape Horn and Tierra del Fuego to Colombia and the Guianas. It also occurs in the southern United States, Europe and Asia.

Cordilleran Snipe

Gallinago stricklandii (G. R. Gray)   A. Becasina grande   C. Becasina gigante
Local name: Jack Snipe ?

IDENTIFICATION. Small-medium. c14″. Heavier, more brightly coloured and having a longer bill (3–3½ in.) than the Common Snipe, this bird is recognized by its *rich reddish-brown back and wings, barred and streaked with black*; black tail barred with red-brown, and *rich buff underparts* unmarked on the belly, but *mottled with black on the breast and barred with black on the flanks*. The bill is brown with a blackish tip. The legs are greyish-yellow.

VOICE. No records are available from the Falkland Is., but on Jerdan and Wollaston Is., south of Tierra del Fuego, P. W. Reynolds (1935) noted that the usual call was 'chip-chip-chip', frequently uttered in flight. It also drummed in flight, producing a very low-pitched whirring note. A loud 'cha-woo, cha-woo, cha-woo' repeated, was also heard from flying birds alternating with the drumming note.

FOOD. No Falkland records, but a female shot by Reynolds at Guffern I. had some beetle remains in the stomach.

HABITAT, STATUS & BREEDING. On the islands near Cape Horn it frequents marshes and peaty ground where rushes are mixed with stunted scrub. In the Falkland Is. it may be found in marshy areas. It is very rare, and there has only been one certain record in recent years. There has been no definite breeding record for many years, and none are documented, although some birds were said to be breeding near Third Corral, east of Port San Carlos some years ago.

DISTRIBUTION ABROAD. It occurs in the Andes of northwestern Venezuela, Colombia and south to western Bolivia, also in southern Tierra del Fuego and islands of the Cape Horn and Magellanic regions. It is less common in southern Chile to 39°S and rare to 37°S.

Least Seedsnipe

Thinocorus rumicivorus Eschscholts
A. Chorlo aperdizado menor   C. Perdicita común

IDENTIFICATION. Very small. 6–7″. This curious bird, only slightly larger than the Black-throated Finch, *resembles a diminutive game-bird on the ground, but in flight resembles a plover.* The male is sandy-brown thickly mottled and barred with black on the crown, back, wing-coverts and central tail feathers. *A broad, black band which separates the white throat from the light grey neck extends down the centre of the neck and broadens again to form a band separating grey neck from white breast and belly.* The dark brown bill is short, broad and curved. The yellow legs are very short. The female is similar above, but has a grey-brown neck and an indistinct black collar. In its rapid flight it shows long narrow pointed wings with blackish primaries and a *short black tail with a broad white tip*, lacking on the central feathers. It is very difficult to see on the ground as its mottled plumage blends well with the grasses and bare earth. Its habits of squatting motionless or running quietly away make it easily overlooked. In South America it is usually seen in pairs or small scattered flocks.

VOICE. When flushed it utters a scraping call like a snipe. On the ground it has a variety of strange calls, resembling pigeons' cooing and like loud taps on hollow ground.

FOOD. It takes small seeds, tender buds and young leaves.

HABITAT, STATUS & BREEDING. Found on open plains and dunes behind beaches in South America, but it is very rare in the Falkland Is., the most recent record being of one seen near Stanley in 1955. It is not known whether this species has bred in the Falkland Is. In South America, the breeding season is extended, eggs being found between August and January. It lays 2–4 creamy, pointed eggs, thickly spotted with reddish-brown, in a scrape on bare earth, sometimes lined or decorated with a little grass or dry dung, with which the eggs are covered during the bird's absence.

DISTRIBUTION ABROAD. The race *Th. r. r.* inhabits Chile from Tierra del Fuego to 27°S and Argentina to about 40°S. In winter it ranges north to about 33°S in Argentina and Uruguay. Two other races are found in the lower Andean regions of northern Argentina, Peru and Bolivia.

Snowy Sheathbill

Chionis alba (Gmelin)   A. & C. Paloma antartica
Local name: Kelp Pigeon

IDENTIFICATION. Medium. c16″. *All white plumage and pigeon-like movements* make this shorebird easily recognizable. The bill is short and stout, coloured green and yellow with a horny sheath round the base, and a brown tip. It looks bleary-eyed due to a patch of bare skin, which is wattled in the adult, below the eye and at the base of the bill. Legs and feet are blue-grey and thick for the size of the bird; the toes are unwebbed but it can swim well when necessary. At

Snowy Sheathbill on Kidney Island.

a distance it can be confused with the male Kelp Goose, but its movements are quicker and in flight it has quick, shallow wing-beats, while head and tail both appear short. Usually silent in the Falkland Is. but parties quarrel amongst themselves over food, uttering short harsh calls. Feeds by scavenging, particularly spilt regurgitated food from penguins and cormorants, and seals' faeces. It also steals eggs.

HABITAT, STATUS & RECORDS. Present round the shores of the Falkland Is. throughout the year but does not breed. Non-breeding immatures are seen in summer at Rockhopper Penguin and King Cormorant colonies and at sea lion rookeries, singly and in groups. In winter, migrants from their breeding-grounds to the south are present in much larger numbers, sometimes in flocks of two to three hundred. One of five banded at George I. in August 1961 by R. Reid was trapped at the British Antarctic Survey base hut on Signy I., South Orkneys in January 1962 and was present in that area for a further three months. A nestling colour-banded at Signy I. during the 1960–1 season was seen at Bleaker I. in December 1961 (Jones, 1963). It is probable that most Sheathbills seen in the Falkland Is. are first year birds or older immatures, as many are present in the Antarctic throughout the winter, and no colour-banded *adults* from Signy I. have been seen in the Falkland Is. Migrants probably reach the Falklands in May and leave in October. Single birds are quite frequently seen hundreds of miles from land.

DISTRIBUTION ABROAD. Breeds at islands of the Scotia Arc from the South Shetlands to South Georgia and also on the coasts of the Antarctic Peninsula to about 65°S. Many migrate to the coasts of the Falkland Is., Tierra del Fuego and Patagonia in winter reaching as far north as the coast of Uruguay. Non-breeding birds are also present throughout the year on the coasts of Tierra del Fuego.

Great Skua

Catharacta skua antarctica (Lesson)   A. Gaviota parda   C. Salteador común
Local name: Sea-hen

IDENTIFICATION. Medium-large. c21″. A *very dark brown seabird*, it is recognized in flight by the *conspicuous white flash near the tip of each wing*, its heavy body and well-pointed wings. The tail is short and slightly rounded. It can be separated at a great distance from a young Kelp Gull as the wings beat more rapidly and travel through a much shallower arc. It appears black against the sky; on the ground it is dark brown flecked with buff on neck and back, lighter grey-brown beneath, sometimes flecked with chestnut on flanks and breast. Some individuals show a yellow-brown hind neck and a dark cap, but plumage colours vary greatly between individuals. The juvenile is darker with few light flecks above. The stout hooked bill is black; legs and feet are also black, but many have mottled white and black tarsi, apparently due to a lack of dark pigment. When chasing other seabirds to make them disgorge, it flies very rapidly with powerful wing-beats, and shows considerable agility. It is notoriously aggressive when nesting, and if eggs or young are threatened, both parents swoop close overhead, calling angrily and sometimes striking men or dogs with the feet.

VOICE. It has various harsh guttural calls, mostly used near the nest or when disputing another's claim to some carrion, but otherwise is usually silent. When confronting another on the ground, the guttural calls are often accompanied by a display, in which both wings are raised high over the back.

FOOD. Obtains much of its food by piratical attacks on other seabirds. In the Falkland Is. it is persistent in terrorising Rock and King Cormorants; it flies nearby when one is diving for fish, then crash-lands at the spot where the cormorant surfaces. It also takes eggs, including those of Cormorants and Upland Geese, as well as young penguins and goslings. It is attracted by offal or sheep carcasses and is said to attack lambs and fallen sheep.

HABITAT, STATUS & BREEDING. A common and widespread summer resident, it is seen in the Falkland Is. between mid-October and late April. It occurs mostly over the surrounding sea, the mainland coasts and on the many off-lying islands, and is rarely seen more than a mile from the sea. It nests colonially on mainland points or on hilltops of the smaller islands, up to half a mile from the sea, but isolated nests are sometimes found. The nest is a scrape scantily lined with grass or diddle-dee pieces in which 2, sometimes only 1, and occasionally 3, very variable greyish, pale green or dark olive-brown eggs, spotted and blotched with dark brown are laid between the end of November and mid-December.

Nearly 150 full-grown and 50 fledgling Skuas were banded mainly at Carcass and Dunbar Is. off West Falkland between 1961 and 1963, but there have been no foreign recoveries. A pair colour-banded at a nest on Kidney I. in December 1961 were seen at exactly the same place in December 1962 and again in mid-March 1963. A juvenile colour-banded at Stanley on 20th March 1962 was seen at Moody Valley Farm ($3\frac{1}{2}$ miles west) on 17th January 1963, having migrated and returned in the interim period.

DISTRIBUTION ABROAD. The race *C. s. antarctica* breeds only in the Falkland Is. In winter it is pelagic, apparently ranging north as far as Brazil (c20°S) and obtains food from various petrels and terns. Closely related races inhabit the coasts of South America, the antarctic continent and sub-antarctic islands from the South Shetlands and South Georgia to New Zealand. Other races occur in arctic regions.

Dolphin Gull

Leucophaeus scoresbii (Traill)   A. Gaviota del Sur   C. Gaviota austral

IDENTIFICATION. Medium. c17″. *Much smaller* than the Kelp Gull, with which it often associates, the adult is identified by its *predominantly grey body, heavy dark red bill and red legs. The back and wings above are slate-black* and the tail is white; the underparts and neck are light grey, also the head between July and February. The adult assumes a dark grey hood briefly from late April to early June and has an intermediate mottled head from mid-March to April and again from late May to early July, although some have regained almost immaculate light grey heads by mid-June. In flight it shows a broad white trailing edge to the wing, and has a characteristic pattern of dark back and wings, light grey body and pure white tail. More daring and much tamer than the Kelp Gull, it will stoop at intruders while screaming loudly, even in winter.

A close study of colour-banded birds over more than three years has shown that the age of most immatures can be determined in the field by the colours of head, bill and legs. Juvenile and first winter birds also have a black terminal bar on the white tail, broadest on the central feathers; these are replaced by white feathers from August in the first winter. In the Table opposite, division of the year into 'Summer' (October–March) and 'Winter' (April–September) is arbitrary. There is obviously some overlap in periods of moult and much individual variation. (Colour photos: p. 171)

VOICE. The flight-note, a short 'kyik', is distinctive; it is much sharper and higher-pitched than most calls of the Kelp Gull. Another commonly heard note, uttered by birds on the ground, at nests or when stooping at an intruder, is a harsh screaming 'keear-keear-keear', repeated quickly.

FOOD. The diet is very varied; it eagerly eats seal faeces and vomited penguin remains in sea lion rookeries, takes offal at slaughterhouses and raw meat thrown to domestic fowls. It also takes regurgitated fish from King Cormorants, penguin eggs, mussels which are dropped from a height of 5–25 ft. onto rocks or the sea wall at Stanley, small black flies which it chases on sand beaches, and

TABLE 4. *Recognition of Immature Dolphin Gulls*

Age	Head	Bill	Legs
Juvenile (Jan.–Mar.)	Dark slate-brown (uniform with throat and upper breast)	Blackish	Dark brown
First Winter	Sooty-grey, mottled white on throat (Breast mottled grey and brown)	Dull pink-brown; tip $\frac{1}{3}$–$\frac{1}{2}$ black	Dark pink-brown
First Summer	Dark grey, mottled dark brown	Pale pink, tip $\frac{1}{3}$ or less black	Dull brown-pink
Second Winter	Sooty-grey, near uniform, sometimes light flecks	Pink; broad black subterminal bar; traces of red	Dark brown, var. red/orange tinge
Second Summer	Mottled dark grey and dark brown on light grey	Pink/Light red; traces of sub-terminal bar	Pale red-brown or orange-red
Third Winter	Dark grey	Light red with darker tip	Dull red-brown
Third Summer	Pale grey as adult	Deep red	Bright red

stranded jellyfish. Occasionally it harries Rock Cormorants, forcing them to fly from a perch and vomit food. It also harries adult Gentoo Penguins when they return to feed their young, and takes scraps around nesting Gentoo and Rockhopper Penguins.

HABITAT, STATUS & BREEDING. A resident, widespread and fairly common around the coast, it is much less numerous than the Kelp Gull. It is particularly attracted to seal, penguin and cormorant colonies where it can find food easily, and flocks gather in winter wherever sheep or cattle have been killed. It breeds in close-packed colonies, usually in association with Kelp Gulls, South American Terns or Brown-hooded Gulls, on sand or shingle beaches and headlands, by ponds in grass or on rocky ridges where nests are sheltered by tussock clumps. Lays in December 2–3 olive-buff or grey-green eggs, well-marked with dark brown blotches. The nest is a hollow, well lined with grass and dead kelp pieces, frequently decorated with pieces of a bright green plant that often grows nearby.

Between June 1959 and January 1963, 239 were banded in the Falkland Is. (Table 5) 134 were banded at Stanley, the Lagoon near Bluff Cove or Kidney I.

Full-grown birds were trapped in Stanley and on Kidney I. beach by single clap-net with mutton bait. The 105 banded in the Camp were divided between Bleaker and George Is. (R. Reid), West Point I. (R. B. Napier) and Carcass I. (D. Galloway).

TABLE 5. *Dolphin Gulls Banded 1959–63*

Station	Full-grown	Fledglings
Stanley	56	—
Kidney I.	12	17
Lagoon	3	46
Bleaker I.	20	—
George I.	34	—
Carcass I.	—	25
West Point I.	26	—
TOTALS	*151*	*88*

74 birds were colour-banded at Stanley, Kidney I. and the Lagoon. Many sight-recoveries were made of these individuals, which revealed, amongst other things, that adults and immatures both have strong tendencies to wander. Eight of 35 fledglings banded at the Lagoon in 1961 were seen, recaptured or killed, at Lively I. (1), Green Patch (1), Kidney I. (1) and Stanley (5). These show dispersal in both directions along the coast of East Falkland (northeast and southwest). Adults also travel quite long distances; one adult banded in Stanley in October 1959 was found dead on the beach at Salvador, 28 miles away by the direct route, eleven months later. Another, banded in August 1961 on George I. (or Bleaker) was seen at Surf Bay the following March, a distance of 93 (or 56) miles to the northeast. Three birds banded as adults were proved to have reached an age of at least seven years when last seen; another was six years old or more. One bird banded in its second winter was five years old when last seen.

DISTRIBUTION ABROAD. This species is restricted to southern South America. It breeds from about 42°S in Chile and Argentina to Tierra del Fuego, and winters as far north as 37°S in both countries.

Kelp Gull

Larus dominicanus Lichtenstein   A. Gaviota cocinera   C. Gaviota dominicana
Local names: Big/White Gull, Grey Gull (first year birds)

IDENTIFICATION. Medium-large. 20–23″. The largest gull breeding in the Falkland Is., it is a familiar bird around Stanley and all the settlements. The

First-year Kelp Gull in a Stanley garden.

adult has *sooty-black mantle and wings above* with a white trailing edge, and *all white head, neck, underparts and tail*, including the under wing-coverts. In winter, from mid-April to mid-September, the adult has a very variable number of dark brown feathers on crown and nape. *The bill is orange-yellow with a bright red gonys patch* and the eyelids are red. Legs and feet are pale greenish-, greyish- or orange-yellow. Adults with orange-yellow legs have deeper orange bills. The *juvenile* looks very dark; it is *heavily mottled and barred dark and light brown*. The wings are dark brown and the tail is mottled, with a terminal black band. *Bill black*; legs dark brown or pink-brown. In its *second winter* it shows variable white on head, underparts and rump, variable slaty feathers on the back and a white tail with black bar. Bill black, but cream at tip and base; legs grey-brown. In its *third winter* it is mainly white on head and underparts, but has a sprinkling of dark feathers on crown, nape and neck. Back and wings are mainly slaty-black; the tail is white with traces of black. Bill pale yellow with traces of orange, a small red patch and variable amount of black subterminally on both mandibles. Legs pale greenish-grey or blue-grey. Adult plumage is attained in the following summer. Although so common round settlements, it is still very wary of man, much more so than the Dolphin Gull. It is often seen in flocks or singly on beaches. (Colour photo: p. 171)

Kelp Gulls waiting over the slaughterhouse outlet pipe in Stanley harbour.

VOICE. A noisy bird, it has many variations on its call-notes. The usual flight-note is a wailing 'keeyoo' repeated over and over again, sometimes very high-pitched and almost a scream with much accent on the first syllable. A note that is often heard from flocks is a sequence resembling laughing, 'kyok-eeyok-eeyok-eeyok'. A completely different 'conversational' note, often heard from a bird investigating a man's presence is a rapid low-pitched 'uk-uk-uk-uk'. The juvenile bird's call is a vibratory descending whistle with a plaintive quality.

FOOD. A successful scavenger that is ready to take advantage of any weakened and dying animals, it is disliked by sheep-farmers for its attacks on fallen sheep and young lambs, but it is certainly performing a useful service by feeding on the sheep carcasses which are annually thrown on the beach or left to rot. In winter numbers of young birds particularly are a nuisance at domestic hen-runs

Kelp Gulls picking over sheep carcasses at the slaughterhouse.

where they take meat thrown out for the hens. It takes any eggs it can find, including those of King Cormorant, Crested Duck, 'Logger' and its neighbours in a colony, as well as killing and eating ducklings and goslings, including 'Logger' ducklings. It also follows shoals of 'krill' offshore and takes starfish, crabs, mussels, limpets, etc., from the intertidal zone, which are often dropped from a height to crack them. In spring it can be seen on grass apparently taking moth larvae from among the roots. From early September most birds desert Stanley for a few weeks, when they patrol the Camp and feed on sheeps' afterbirths and new-born lambs.

HABITAT, STATUS & BREEDING. One of the most abundant birds in the Falkland Is., it is found on sand beaches, around settlements, over offshore kelp beds and often seen flying over the Camp far from the sea. It is a resident, but

Kelp Gulls over the colony on Carcass Island.

both old and young birds disperse from the breeding grounds and tend to gather where food is plentiful in the winter. In 1833/4 when Charles Darwin visited the Falkland Is. he may have seen this species, but makes no mention of its abundance or habits in these islands. Abbott, writing in 1860, reported that it was a common breeding bird, but apparently migratory as he only saw a few adults in winter. By the early 20th century, Cobb (1910) found it to be the commonest gull, well-known for its scavenging and predatory habits. The Kelp Gull, without much doubt, increased as the sheep-farming industry expanded. In 1833 the sheep population was negligible; in 1860 there were only about 10,000 in the Islands, whereas by 1910 they had increased to about 724,000, one of the highest numbers that Falkland pastures have carried. The Kelp Gull is now abundant, resident throughout the year and obviously dependent to a great extent on the whole sheep-farming process. It nests in colonies, often several hundred pairs, although single nests are found. Colonies may be on shingle beaches, eroded sandy ridges, or on diddle-dee and grass-covered slopes. The nests, bulky untidy structures of grass, diddle-dee or kelp pieces, are irregularly spaced in the colony, rarely less than 6 ft. apart. Lays 2–3 eggs, very variable in colour, from olive-green to blue-grey or rich buff-brown well spotted and blotched with dark brown. Most eggs are laid during the first half of December. The juveniles are flying strongly and desert the colonies with their parents early in March.

Over 1300 were banded in the Falkland Is. between 1959 and 1964, the majority (over 900) being trapped by single clap-nets at Stanley. About 120 were caught during the winter of 1961 in a hen-run at Darwin School. 280 fledglings were banded; 178 at the Lagoon near Bluff Cove between 1960 and 1963, and 102 at Carcass I. in 1962. No foreign recoveries have been reported. The longest movement proved was that made by a fledgling banded on Carcass I. on 5th February 1962 and trapped in Stanley six months later, a straight distance of 120 miles. 18 others banded in Stanley were found dead; 11 in Stanley, 5 within a radius of 3 miles, 1 at Cape Pembroke Light 8 miles distant and 1 at Port Louis 18 miles away. 84 fledglings were banded at the Lagoon in January 1962, and three movements have been reported. One bird reached Swan Inlet, about 23 miles westsouthwest within four months. Two occurred in Stanley, 10 miles eastnortheast, one after six months and the other three years after banding. An adult colour-banded in Stanley in May 1960 was seen repeatedly on the same stretch of the sea wall opposite the Secretariat during the winters of 1960, 1961 and 1962, usually accompanied by another smaller bird, presumably its mate. On 16th December 1961 it was seen at the Lagoon colony, 10 miles westsouthwest of Stanley. From the above and other observations, it can be inferred that adults have certain favoured winter feeding areas to which they regularly return. It also appears that pairs remain together throughout the winter.

DISTRIBUTION ABROAD. *L. dominicanus* has a very wide latitudinal range in South America. It breeds from southern Brazil (23°S) and Peru (6°S) through Chile, Uruguay and Argentina (mainly on the coasts) to Tierra del Fuego. It also breeds on the South Shetlands, South Georgia and the Antarctic Peninsula to about 68°S. Apart from this wide range it has an extensive circumpolar distribution in the sub-antarctic zone and breeds at most sub-antarctic islands, in New Zealand and on the coasts of South Africa.

Brown-hooded Gull

Larus maculipennis Lichtenstein
A. Gaviota capucho pardo   C. Gaviota cagüil
Local name: Pink-breasted Gull

IDENTIFICATION. Small-medium. c15″. The *smallest* and least common Falkland gull, it has a *pearly-grey back and wings with a characteristic white leading edge to the primaries*. The underparts are white with a variable roseate suffusion on neck, breast and even the wing edge and tail, which is probably brightest in winter. The undersides of the primaries are dark grey and the primary tips are black. In breeding plumage, acquired from July to August and retained till February, *the whole head is dark chocolate-brown*; *in winter plumage the head is white* with a few dark spots behind the eye. The slender bill is dark crimson; the legs and feet brighter crimson. The *juvenile* is mottled brown on back, wings and crown, shows a narrow black trailing edge to the wing, but still has the white leading edge; the tail is white with a thin black terminal bar. In *first winter* plumage the back and wing-coverts are grey but some brown coverts are retained. The bills of juveniles and first winter birds are light orange-red with a black tip; the legs are light yellow-brown. In the summer following its first winter the dark hood is incomplete. *Flight* is buoyant with *shallow beats*; it can be separated from the South American Tern even at a long distance by its much shorter, broader wings, with black undersides to the primaries. Flocks at their nesting grounds and in winter, will often mob a human intruder, calling continuously.

VOICE. The usual flight-note is a short 'kip' lower-pitched than the South American Tern's call. A harsh guttural 'kwarr' is used when mobbing or at the nest.

FOOD. Its favourite feeding places are on the kelp beds, where it takes small fishes and other marine organisms. It also feeds by picking small objects, probably sandhoppers or drifted 'krill' from the surf edge. It is sometimes seen 'treading' waterlogged sand on beaches, and occasionally will take meat around settlements in winter. In South America, it is a familiar bird at slaughterhouses and poultry runs, but it is rarely seen at such places in the Falkland Is., possibly because its three competitors (Kelp and Dolphin Gulls and Skuas) are much stronger, and the Kelp Gull far more numerous.

HABITAT, STATUS & BREEDING. A resident species, only locally common, it is often overlooked as its usual haunts, out of the breeding season, are the extensive kelp beds. It breeds in colonies of up to a hundred pairs in lake reed-beds or on small islands (up to 3 miles inland), on open rocky peninsulas or shingle points, often with a Dolphin Gull or South American Tern colony. A colony of about twenty pairs on Kidney I., examined in December 1961 and 1962 was situated about 40 ft. above the sea on a narrow steep-sided outlier. The nests of dry grass were placed on and between small tussock clumps, most being so close together that it was difficult to step between them. It lays 2–3, occasionally 4 eggs, of an olive or buff colour, heavily blotched with brown. It nests slightly later than other Falkland gulls, laying from the third week of December to early January.

ABOVE Adult Dolphin Gull flying above adult Kelp Gull, Lagoon, near Bluff Cove, East Falkland (*see p.* 162).
BELOW Dolphin Gulls at nests, Bold Point, East Falkland.

DISTRIBUTION ABROAD. This species is widely distributed in southern South America, breeding on the coasts and inland from Tierra del Fuego north to Chile and to northeast Argentina and Uruguay (33°S). It breeds in Argentina only in the eastern and southern provinces, ranging north and west in winter, when it also reaches 18°S in Chile and 10°S in eastern Brazil.

South American Tern

Sterna hirundinacea Lesson
A. Gaviotín cola larga   C. Gaviotín sud-americano
Local names: Split-tailed or Swallow-tailed Gull

IDENTIFICATION. Medium. c16″. The only tern breeding in the Falkland Is., it is a beautiful *slender almost white bird with long thin pointed wings*. The adult has a *jet-black cap from bill to nape* with a thin white line below it; upper surface including the wings, pale pearly-grey, underparts somewhat lighter becoming white on the belly. *Tail white, deeply forked, with long streamers on the outer feathers.* Bill fairly heavy and sharply pointed, bright blood-red; legs and feet also bright red. The *juvenile* lacks tail streamers, has a black bar on the forewing and scapulars, brown mottled back, black bill and pink legs. A *first year bird* has whitish forehead, blackish bill and dull red legs, and a blackish 'V' on the lesser wing-coverts. In *flight* its most noticeable features are the jerky action of the very long thin wings lifting the body at each stroke, and the long trailing tail. It is often seen fishing in large loose flocks over kelp beds, diving vertically into water from about 20 ft. It also hovers and then drops to the surface to pick up food. When breeding it is antagonistic to 'Caranchos', Skuas, Kelp Gulls and man, often stooping close to a man's head and sometimes even striking with the feet.

VOICE. In flight it often uses a short clear 'kyik', sharper and higher pitched than the Brown-hooded Gull's call. When mobbing it utters a harsh, descending scream, 'keceerr' or a short 'ik-ik-ik'. At the nesting grounds it is very noisy, the air being constantly filled by their harsh cries. A pair standing together on rocks in Stanley harbour uttered quiet, conversational notes, a harsh 'kuk-kuk' and a triple 'kucherkuk'.

FOOD. Small fish and crustaceans are the staple diet, obtained by diving or by picking them from the surface of kelp beds.

HABITAT, STATUS & BREEDING. A common summer visitor, it arrives from late September to October and leaves in March and early April (earliest 29th

ABOVE Brown-hooded Gull, adult (*see p.* 169).

BELOW Brown-hooded Gulls and South American Terns over mixed colony, Seal Point, East Falkland.

September; latest 11th April). It is widespread round the Falkland Is., most often seen over the kelp beds, but also in the lower reaches of the larger rivers. Breeds in colonies, often with Brown-hooded Gulls or near Dolphin or Kelp Gulls on a variety of sites, but mostly on shingle or rocky beaches and peninsulas, or on isolated rock points sheltered by tussock-grass or thrift. On beaches the nests are merely scrapes, but where grasses and thrift are available, the scrape is well lined. Single nests are also found and it sometimes nests at freshwater ponds; one large colony in Island Harbour camp in 1963 was 3 miles inland, and food was carried to the young from the sea. It lays 2 eggs of very variable shape and colour, ranging from buff to pale blue and rich olive-brown, variably speckled and blotched with brown. The eggs are smaller than those of the Brown-hooded Gull. Eggs are laid between the end of November and late December, and fledged young may be seen from late January.

DISTRIBUTION ABROAD. It is a common breeding bird on both coasts of South America from islands of Cape Horn and Tierra del Fuego to 14°S in Peru and to 23°S in Brazil. It ranges northward on migration to 7°S on the Peruvian coast and to 13°S on the Brazilian coast.

South American Tern at Gipsy Cove.

Eared Dove

Zenaida auriculata (Des Murs)   A. Paloma torcaza   C. Tortola común

IDENTIFICATION. Small. c$10\frac{1}{2}$". The only wild pigeon occurring with any regularity in the Falkland Is., it is recognized on the ground by its *small size, generally grey-brown plumage above with a few large black spots on scapulars and wing-coverts*, and short reddish legs. It has a pale grey crown and flanks, light brown neck and breast with two indistinct black bars by the ear-coverts, a shiny purple area at the side of the neck, and a whitish belly. When flushed it rises rapidly, with its graduated grey-brown tail fanned, showing white edging and a narrow black subterminal band.

HABITAT, STATUS & RECORDS. A ground-feeding bird that occurs occasionally in gardens and near settlements in the Falkland Is. Single birds, sometimes two together, have been recorded about twenty times, mainly during the autumn, in March. Also seen in February, April, June and once in September/October when one bird survived in gardens at Stanley at least from 20th September to 13th October 1961. Most individuals seem to find abundant food, such as corn thrown out for domestic fowls and garden weed seeds. They could possibly survive successfully but for the too plentiful semi-wild cats.

DISTRIBUTION ABROAD. The race *Z. a. auriculata* is common in central and southern Chile from 30–47°S and in the southern half of Argentina. It is occasional in Tierra del Fuego and the Magellanic region. Another race inhabits the rest of Argentina, Uruguay, Bolivia and the southern parts of Brazil.

Barn Owl

Tyto alba tuidara (Gray)   A. Lechuza de los campanarios   C. Lechuza blanca

IDENTIFICATION. Small-medium. c14". *Orange-buff back and wings*, mottled and flecked with grey and white, *mainly white underparts and conspicuous white heart-shaped facial disc* separate this owl from the slightly larger Short-eared Owl. The underparts are frequently suffused with buff on breast and flanks and often well spotted with grey. The rather long legs are thickly covered with white feathers. Typical call used in flight is an eerie scream; it also makes hissing and snoring noises.

HABITAT, STATUS & RECORDS. Only three certain records, all of single birds; one shot in the Johnson's Harbour area, probably in the 1940s; one killed at Cape Pembroke Light on 14th September 1937 (the skin now in the British

Museum); one caught alive at George I. in July 1963 and later released in Stanley. These were probably all vagrants from South America, but reports of 'white owls' breeding in Port Howard camp at Shag Cove opposite Swan I., and at Mt. Caroline near Port Purvis, which were received by E. M. Cawkell in 1951, possibly refer to this species.

DISTRIBUTION ABROAD. Very widely distributed throughout the world, this species, *Tyto alba*, and its several races are found in most continents. *T. a. tuidara* breeds in South America from the Guianas and eastern Peru through Brazil, Chile, Uruguay and Argentina to Tierra del Fuego.

Burrowing Owl

Speotyto cunicularia (Molina)
A. Lechucita de las vizcacheras   C. Pequén

IDENTIFICATION. Small. c10". *A small owl, light brown above mottled with white;* creamy-white below with *a blackish collar across the neck.* The facial disc is brown with white 'eyebrows'. The iris is yellow. It has rather long legs. A ground-loving bird of open country, that typically perches on a hillock during the day and calls shrilly as intruders approach. It also frequently flies by day.

HABITAT, STATUS & RECORDS. One certain record only; a dead bird found on West Falkland in late November 1945. Eggs have been found in short burrows in the white grass at Island Harbour, East Falkland in the 1950s and at Fox Bay, West Falkland in 1955, which were possibly of this species. It is therefore possible that the Burrowing Owl breeds, although no more have been reported since 1945. The undulating white grass Camp would appear to be a suitable habitat.

DISTRIBUTION ABROAD. *S. cunicularia* is represented in South America except Brazil, by three races. *S. c. cunicularia*, the southern type, occurs commonly in Chile from 18–40°S and in Paraguay, Uruguay and most of Argentina, except the high Andes of the northwest, from 23°S to Tierra del Fuego (55°S).

Rufous-legged Owl

Strix rufipes rufipes King   A. Lechuza bataraz   C. Concón común

IDENTIFICATION. Small-medium. c14". This owl is easily distinguished from the Short-eared by its dark brown head and heavily barred plumage. The back and wings are dark brown barred with buff and red-brown; *the underparts are heavily barred with dark brown on buff-white. The underside of the tail is broadly barred with black and white.* A little-known species in Chile, but for its loud hooting call, it inhabits woods and forests and is completely nocturnal. It feeds principally on mice and other small animals.

HABITAT, STATUS & RECORDS. Although reputed to breed on Hill Cove and Port Howard farms, there are no breeding records and it is unlikely that a bird of the South American forests would inhabit the naturally treeless Falkland Is. No records of *S. r.* in the Falkland Is. could be found in the literature consulted and there have been no records in the past forty years. Bennett preserved the skin of an owl that struck Cape Pembroke Light in September 1937, but it was wrongly labelled '*Strix rufipes*'. It was a Barn Owl, *Tyto alba tuidara*, and is now in the British Museum.

DISTRIBUTION ABROAD. *S. r. rufipes*, the typical race, inhabits southern South America from 33°S in Chile and from about 38°S in Argentina to Tierra del Fuego. Another race is found in Paraguay and the northern parts of Argentina to about 37°S.

Short-eared Owl

Asio flammeus sanfordi Bangs   A. Lechuzón de los campos   C. Nuco

IDENTIFICATION. Small-medium. 14–15″. The only owl common in the Falkland Is., it is recognized by its *dark brown back, wings and tail beautifully mottled and barred with buff, and rich buff underparts widely streaked on the breast with dark brown.* When perched it shows a conspicuous light buff, rounded facial disc edged with white below, and large orange- or lemon-yellow eyes circled with black feathers. The legs are covered with buff feathers; the claws and bill are dark horn or blackish. In flight it is easily recognized by *long broad and round-ended wings, large rounded head,* short tail and characteristic *deep and slow wing-beats* with a wavering action. It flies low over the ground when hunting and is most active around dusk and till at least midnight in late December, but it also flies by day and sometimes at a considerable height (up to 100 ft.).

VOICE. Usually silent except during the breeding season when adults utter a sharp 'yip-yip-yip' and a sneezing 'wheechiz' as they circle over intruders. Also in the breeding season (noted up to 31st October) it has a circling display-flight in which it claps the wings sharply together and drops suddenly while uttering a repeated low 'boo-boo-boo'. This 'song' is also uttered when the bird is perched.

FOOD. Takes large numbers of Grey-backed Storm-Petrels, Diving Petrels and probably Slender-billed Prions during the spring and summer. It also takes large weevils found on diddle-dee, the wingless Camel-crickets found on tussock islands, and has been known to take Tussock-birds. Birds occasionally seen round Stanley in winter may take House Sparrows and rats.

HABITAT, STATUS & BREEDING. This owl is widely distributed around the Falkland Is., but only locally common on some of the larger islands and tussock islands, where it usually breeds. It may be seen over the Camp during the winter, where there is a good cover of long grass. Nests on the ground in the shelter of thick grass, particularly cinnamon grass or in tussock-grass or rushes. The eggs are white and rounded; Pettingill (1958) reports the clutch-size as 2. It probably lays in September. A juvenile has been seen in early November, but there are no published Falkland breeding records.

DISTRIBUTION ABROAD. The race *A. f. sanfordi* is confined to the Falkland Is. Other races occur in most parts of the world, except New Zealand and Australia. The South American race *A. f. suinda* is widespread and fairly common from Venezuela, the Guianas and Brazil through Argentina and Chile to Tierra del Fuego.

Short-eared Owl in flight.

Short-eared Owl.

Tussock-bird investigating the hut on Kidney Island.

Blackish Cinclodes / Tussock-bird

Cinclodes a. antarcticus (Garnot)   A. Piloto negro   C. Churrete austral
Local name: Black Bird

IDENTIFICATION. Small. c8″. This tame, restless bird can be immediately recognized as it is the only *small* Falkland bird with *all dark brown plumage*, apart from buff flecks on the throat and sides of the neck. *The mainly black bill* with a varying amount of yellow at the base, *is rather long and slightly down-curved*; the legs are black. The juvenile resembles the adult but has more yellow at the base of the bill and a yellow gape. The flight is rapid with quick beats of fairly long and broad wings showing a red-brown bar across the inner primaries and secondaries. It flies just above the tussock-grass, shooting down slopes with few wing-beats between long glides. *It is remarkably tame and inquisitive*, often approaching close to a man and even perching on his foot or shoulder, but is very pugnacious to others of its own species in the breeding season. It has a low stance and runs rapidly when feeding on beaches. A peculiar musty odour is apparent when the bird is handled.

VOICE. The call-note is a short sharp 'chip' uttered singly or repeated. In chases the call rises in pitch and becomes a rapid trill, 'chee-chee-chee-chee . . .' ending with harsher lower notes, 'chur-chur-chur'. The song, of similar notes, is uttered from a perch or the ground, accompanied by raised and fluttered wings. The wing-raising display may be seen throughout the year, apparently indicating aggressive intentions towards other Tussock-birds and to other species. There is little information on the song-period, but it probably sings mostly between September and January.

FOOD. It has a varied diet ranging from small marine invertebrates picked from the surf edge or amongst heaps of rotted kelp to blow-flies, worms and large Camel-crickets; it also takes regurgitated fish from King and Rock Cormorants, household scraps, crumbs, mutton and mutton fat at settlements. It will even enter houses to take butter from a dish on a table. Partially digested regurgitated fish from cormorants and Camel-crickets are commonly fed to young in the nest.

HABITAT, STATUS & BREEDING. A very common resident species on those outer islands that do not support rats or cats, it is a bird of the sand and boulder beaches, particularly where kelp accumulates above high water mark. It is not restricted to tussock islands although it is abundant on islands where this grass is dominant. It may occasionally be seen on mainland beaches. Its distribution before the mainland coastal fringes of tussock disappeared is unknown, but it may have inhabited such areas near suitable beaches. It nests from early September till December, though most start laying in October. It is usually double-brooded. The nest, which has a shallow cup, is made of dry grass lined with a few feathers and may be placed in a hole under a shed, up to 2 ft. below the surface of loose rocks on a beach, in an earth bank or an old burrow of the Diving Petrel. It lays 1–3 slightly glossy white eggs, sometimes minutely spotted with red round the blunt end.

About 180 were banded between 1959 and 1963, 85 at Kidney I. and most of the remainder at George I. Only 41 were colour-banded at Kidney, but from sight-recoveries it was found that adults tended to remain in their nesting territories from October to mid-April, although during the breeding season they would cross the island (c300 yds.) to collect food for their young from the King Cormorant colony. Four birds were proved to reach $3\frac{1}{2}$ years of age, while two of these were last seen at an age of around 5 years.

DISTRIBUTION ABROAD. The race *C. a. antarcticus* is restricted to the Falkland Is. The other race, *C. a. maculirostris* occurs only on islands south of Tierra del Fuego and at Staten I. east of Tierra del Fuego.

Dark-faced Ground-tyrant

Muscisaxicola macloviana macloviana (Garnot)
A. Dormilona cabeza parda   C. Dormilona tontito
Local names: Blue Bird, News Bird

IDENTIFICATION. Very small. c6½″. A slim, sprightly little bird, *pale grey-brown above with a darker brown head, grey-white below with long black legs* and a short pointed black bill. *The tail, which is black with a narrow white outer edge,* is repeatedly flicked and fanned in one quick movement and the wings are also flicked at each momentary pause in the bird's travels. It has black lores, a dark eye and variable dark chestnut on the crown and chin. The flight feathers are dark brown with white edges, noticeable when it is perched. Although they look alike, the male is slightly larger than the female. The juvenile has a yellow gape and orange-yellow bill with a dark brown tip. It runs and hops rapidly and its flight is swift and easy with quick beats of its rather long wings. It has an upright stance and always chooses the highest perch available after a flight. Sometimes darts from an elevated perch after flies and frequently hovers before dropping a few feet to the ground when searching for food over long grass. It is seen singly or in pairs, but in winter small parties travel in loose association.

VOICE. The usual call-note, frequently uttered, is a short squeaky 'tseet'. It also has a low hard note 'tu', which may be repeated rapidly or combined with the first note, 'seetu'. It also has a weak twittering song which is rarely heard. In September and October the male displays to the female on the ground, singing and raising one or both wings slowly to about 60° from horizontal then closing them, repeating the movements frequently. In these positions the bird resembles a butterfly sunning itself. It also has a display-flight in which it mounts to about 50 ft. like a Pipit, then drops quickly to a rock.

FOOD. It takes various small insects, such as black 'sand-flies', blow-flies, small moths and their larvae and worms, on which the young are also fed.

HABITAT, STATUS & BREEDING. A common resident throughout the islands, it is found wherever there are rocky outcrops or stone-runs inland and on coastal cliffs and sand beaches with heaps of kelp. It also frequents gardens in Stanley and the settlements in winter. It nests between late October and late December laying 2–3 slightly glossy white eggs, closely spotted with red-brown, in a cup-shaped nest of dry grass or root fibres well lined with wool or feathers (e.g. those of 'Loggers' or domestic fowls). The nest is often built in a stone-run, sheltered about 2 ft. below the surface, but may be in a deep crevice on a rocky ridge or cliff by the sea. It is probably double-brooded.

Dark-faced Ground-tyrant.

Three only were trapped and banded between 1959 and 1963 mainly because it seems capable of seeing and avoiding a mist-net when Falkland Thrushes and Tussock-birds fly straight into the net. It also has the annoying habit of perching on the top strand of the net or on one of the mist-net poles. One colour-banded on Kidney I. in 1959 was at least 4 years old when last seen there in 1962.

DISTRIBUTION ABROAD. The race *M. m. macloviana* is apparently restricted to the Falkland Is., although Olrog (1959, p. 224) considers that it migrates to northeast Argentina in winter. The race *M. m. mentalis* breeds in southern Chile from 42°S and Argentina from 30°S to Tierra del Fuego and Cape Horn. In winter it migrates north to 12°S in Peru and to 22°S in northwest Argentina.

Chilean Swallow

Tachycineta leucopyga (Meyen)
A. Golondrina azul   C. Golondrina de rabadilla blanca

IDENTIFICATION. Minute. c5½″. *A black and white swallow with a prominent white rump*, all black head and short, slightly forked black tail. Black back, wings and head show a metallic blue sheen; white on the throat extends behind the black ear-coverts forming a short half collar; underparts are white with brown shading at the sides of breast and flanks. The flight silhouette of triangular wing-spread and short tail is typical, and quite unlike that of the Barn Swallow. Flies with few wing-beats between long glides.

HABITAT, STATUS & RECORDS. First noted in the Falkland Is. on 6th March 1937 when J. E. Hamilton obtained one immature specimen from a flock of six or seven. An exhausted specimen was picked up on Kidney I. on 24th February 1954 by O. S. Pettingill jr. Recorded annually from 1958 to 1962 inclusive in and around Stanley, particularly along John Street, where tall cypress and willow wind-breaks provide shelter and harbour flies and gnats. It occurs in the Falkland Is. as a vagrant from the Magellanic region of South America, when they are migrating northwards in the autumn. It has been recorded from mid-February to early June, but most appear between mid-March and early May; it has not been recorded in the spring. Two individuals survived for at least one month, between 9th April and 9th May 1958, when they were seen frequently along the sheltered part of John Street.

DISTRIBUTION ABROAD. Breeds in southern Chile and Argentina from Tierra del Fuego north to 27°S in Chile and 37°S in Argentina. It is resident in central and south-central Chile throughout the year, but those breeding in the most southerly regions migrate northwards in winter, when it is found in Argentina, Paraguay and southern Brazil.

Southern Martin

Progne modesta elegans Baird   A. & C. Golondrina negra

IDENTIFICATION. Small. c8½″. Distinguished immediately from the other two swallows occurring in the Falkland Is. by its *greater size, deeply forked tail and very dark plumage*. The male is black with purple and blue sheen; the female is dark grey with less sheen, but immature birds, probably resembling the female, are more likely to reach the Falkland Is.

HABITAT, STATUS & RECORDS. An occasional vagrant at spring and autumn migration periods; it could be seen almost anywhere, but is more likely to occur around settlements with planted trees. The most recent record is of three and five in Stanley and twelve at Cape Pembroke during the same week of March 1951.

DISTRIBUTION ABROAD. The race *P. m. elegans* is found in southern Bolivia (17°S), Uruguay and Argentina from Jujuy to Chubut (46°S) and also occurs very occasionally in central Chile. It is a summer visitor in the southern parts of its range. Another race, *P. m. murphyi*, inhabits the coastal parts of Peru.

Barn Swallow

Hirundo rustica erythrogaster Boddaert
A. Golondrina tijereta   C. Golondrina bermeja

IDENTIFICATION. Very small. c7″. The Barn Swallow's long wings, forked tail and rapid easy flight soon attract attention when it occurs in the Falkland Is. The adult is *blue-black above, has chestnut forehead and throat*, blue-black band across the breast and *buff underparts. The tail is deeply forked*, the outer feathers being much elongated to form streamers, and all except the central pair show *white patches on the inner web* near the tip. A first year bird lacks the tail streamers, is duller and more brown above with paler buff on the head, a broken dark breast band and paler underparts.

HABITAT, STATUS & RECORDS. May be seen almost anywhere over the Islands, but it is particularly attracted to the vicinity of houses and planted trees, where flies are more likely to be available. It occurs annually as a wind-blown vagrant in the southern spring and early summer, mainly during October and November, occasionally in September (earliest 20th September 1962) and January (latest 25th January 1959). Rarely occurs in autumn (three records between early March and mid-April). Single birds or small parties up to five are usual, but forty were seen once at New I. It is often reported from widely separated localities on almost the same date, which suggests that quite large numbers are drifted from the South American coast at one time. Most specimens handled or watched closely have been first year birds. Barn Swallows do not survive for long in the Falkland Is., due to a shortage of food in the form of flying insects and a lack of shelter from the generally strong winds. The longest recorded survival is of eleven days, when five first seen on 8th October 1960 at the Monstar Hotel, east of Stanley, had decreased to two by 19th October.

DISTRIBUTION ABROAD. *H. r. erythrogaster* is the North American breeding race of the species which is found throughout Europe and Asia to northern India and Japan. This race migrates southward through Central and South America and winters (August–May) in Argentina and Chile south to Tierra del Fuego.

Short-billed Marsh Wren / Grass Wren

Cistothorus platensis falklandicus Chapman
A. Ratona aperdizada   C. Chercán de las vegas
Local name: Tomtit

IDENTIFICATION. Very minute. $4\frac{1}{2}$–5″. This wren is distinguished from the slightly larger House Wren by its generally lighter plumage, with *all the upperparts clearly striated buff and black* and the tail barred black and red-brown. It has *a noticeable buff eye-stripe, a pale brownish bill shorter than that of the House Wren* and flesh coloured legs. The underparts are creamy-buff with whitish cheeks and throat. The juvenile is darker, with reddish-buff underparts and an indistinct eye-stripe. It is very active and adept at vanishing through thick vegetation. The flight is weak and slow with whirring wing-beats, usually just above the grass tops, but it is reluctant to fly unless hard pressed. It is inquisitive and often perches on top of a grass clump with tail cocked up and bobs at an intruder while craning its head and neck, but it is not as tame as the House Wren. (Colour photo: p. 189)

VOICE. The usual call-note is a clear hard 'tak-tak' or 'tit-tit', frequently repeated and often run together as a harsh trill, 'trrrr'. The song is much longer than that of the House Wren, usually with a slower delivery; it is composed of a repetition of different clear notes, 'sioo-sioo-sioo', 'chiwi-chiwi-chiwi' and 'clee-clee-clee', separated by short low trills, the whole song frequently being sustained for a minute or more with few brief intervals. It sings from the top of grass clumps and often takes off and whirrs away horizontally to another clump singing continuously. The song has been heard from early September to mid-March.

FOOD. Probably small insects; there are few records available, but it has been seen carrying a small caterpillar and a large fly to its young.

HABITAT, STATUS & BREEDING. A widespread resident, fairly common in its own favourite habitats, which are thick rush patches, long white grass and diddle-dee near ponds and streams or where the ground is permanently damp. It is also found on tussock-covered islands; on Kidney I. it is less common than the House Wren and rarely leaves the grass cover to hunt food on the boulder beach. The nest is a ball of grasses 4 to 8 in. in diameter, occasionally as much as 24 in., well lined with wool and feathers; it is built in bushes, rushes or grass about 1 ft. above the ground. It has a small round entrance on one side and sometimes a grass tunnel is constructed leading to the entrance. It lays 5–7 pure white eggs between early October and mid-November; there is no evidence that it rears more than one brood.

A few were banded on Kidney I. between 1958 and 1963. Two were retrapped almost exactly where they were originally trapped after intervals of a year in each case.

DISTRIBUTION ABROAD. The race *C. p. falklandicus* is only found in the Falkland Is. Other races inhabit Guyana, Venezuela, Colombia, most of Argentina and Chile to Tierra del Fuego and Cape Horn.

Southern House Wren

Troglodytes aedon cobbi Chubb   A. Ratona común   C. Chercán común
Local name: Rock Wren

IDENTIFICATION. Minute. c5¼″. A *tiny, plump, brown-grey bird* with a rather long, slightly curved dark bill and *short tail, usually cocked up*. It is separated from the Grass Wren by its *uniform dark chestnut back*, grey-brown head, buff-white underparts and *total lack of striations*. The underparts are sometimes suffused with buff. The wings and tail are bright chestnut finely barred with dark brown. The juvenile has a darker head and richer body colour. Some birds seen on Kidney I. had a noticeable white patch above the eye and one with symmetrical white flank patches was caught in March 1963, but these are probably slight plumage aberrations in a small isolated population. It is very tame, but vanishes silently into the grass when disturbed in preference to flying. On rocky beaches it slips between and under large boulders like a mouse.

VOICE. The usual song is loud and consists of a mixed phrase of quick trills and whistles with harsh notes, rapidly delivered and lasting about two seconds with regular intervals of three to four seconds. Song varies greatly between individuals. One bird sang only a slow trill repeated at ten second intervals; another elaborated the normal song into a continuous warbling lasting about twenty seconds. It sings mainly from late August to February, but snatches of song have been heard in mid-April. The call-notes are all harsh and buzzing, commonly 'chiz' or 'chiz-iz' or a higher 'cheez'. These notes are quite different from the Grass Wren's usual calls. When it is excited, calls become very loud and explosive.

FOOD. It feeds on small insects and lice found under beach rocks; it also takes crickets and has been recorded apparently feeding on tussock seed-heads. Nestlings are fed on small caterpillars.

HABITAT, STATUS & BREEDING. It is restricted to the outer islands with or without tussock-grass, where it favours boulder beaches. It is common on islands where no cats or rats are present. It breeds between October and December and is probably double-brooded. The nest, made of grasses with a deep cup well-lined with large soft feathers of Turkey Vulture or any others available, may be built in a variety of well-hidden sites, such as a hole in a tussock clump, amongst dead tussock stems or in a rock crevice; occasionally in unnatural sites, such as a sheepskin hanging on a fence. 3–4 eggs are laid, of a pinkish colour, thickly spotted with red or light brown.

One nest from Kidney I. built in a cavity 2 ft. off the ground in the basal pedestal of a tussock clump and containing young in October 1962, was examined in January 1963. The main outer structure was dry grass stems 7 to 8 in. long, although a few were up to 13 in. long. The grasses were woven in a circle intermixed with root fibres, feathers and seals' hairs. Most of the inner material was root fibres, but feathers almost equalled them in bulk. The nest contained about 100 seals' hairs and 255 feathers of at least seven species. 171 of the feathers (28 flank, 133 breast or back, 5 secondaries and 5 tail) were of the Grey-backed Storm-Petrel, whose corpses are often found where Short-

ABOVE Adult male Long-tailed Meadowlark at Stanley (*see p.* 196).
CENTRE Grass Wren near Mullet Creek, East Falkland (*see p.* 186).
BELOW Adult male Falkland Thrush, Stanley (*see p.* 191).

eared Owls have left them on the ground or on tussock pedestals. 31 breast, back and neck feathers of the Turkey Vulture were counted, and 19 feathers of the Falkland Thrush (17 breast or back and 2 tail), 11 downy feathers of the Short-eared Owl and 2 bastard-wing feathers of the Diving Petrel. There were also 2 penguin feathers, 1 probably from the Night Heron and 18 which could not be identified. Curiously, no feathers of the Tussock-bird were included, though this bird is very common on Kidney I.

DISTRIBUTION ABROAD. The race *T. a. cobbi* is restricted to the Falkland Is. Other races inhabit most of tropical and temperate North and South America.

Falkland Thrush

Turdus f. falcklandii   Quoy et Gaimard
A. Zorzal patagónico   C. Zorzal común
Local name: Thrush, American name: Falkland Robin

IDENTIFICATION. Small. 10–10½″. This plump robust bird is easily recognized by its *brown and black plumage, strong orange bill* and fairly long orange-yellow legs. The *adult* is olive-brown on back and wing-coverts with dark brown flight feathers, black tail and contrasting yellow-grey rump. The mantle and neck are lighter olive-buff while the breast is rich buff and the throat is closely streaked cream and black. The head is darker than the back; the *adult male* is mainly black on the crown, nape and round the eye, while the *female* has a dark reddish-brown crown and no black on the nape, but head colours vary and many pairs are indistinguishable. The adults' plumage also fades considerably between October and December. Both sexes have a stout pointed, bright orange-yellow bill, variably streaked with dark brown, but it is mainly brown in autumn. The *juvenile* is streaked with buff above and has *buff underparts heavily spotted with black* on breast and flanks, but breast and neck feathers rapidly become whitish through fading. Although most spotted feathers are moulted in January and February, some individuals still have a few in mid-April and some buff-tipped median coverts are often retained till the following November. The bill is mainly brown and the legs are dull yellow-brown. It has an alert upright stance, often holding the wings loosely with tips drooping well below either side of the tail. Usually hops or bounds over the ground, but can run fast when necessary. It flicks the tail up once or twice each time it stops or alights on a perch. It is aggressive towards its own and other smaller species, and towards man when it has young. Its loud harsh calls and use of prominent high perches

ABOVE Fox Pt. East Falkland, looking west up Choiseul Sound. Only one pedestal remains from the former strip of luxuriant tussock-grass (*see p.* 22).
BELOW On top of Mt. Misery, West Point I. Re-established grasses in the foreground. Wind-eroded ground beyond (*see p.* 30).

make it easily noticed. Usually seen singly or in pairs, but from January parties of young birds gather (sometimes with adults in winter) and are maintained till about August when territories are established. In Stanley, one such party of about ten birds roosted socially in a dense gorse patch.

VOICE. It has various call-notes, most of them loud and harsh, ranging from a thin vibratory 'sreep' to a strong 'choyz-choyz-choyz' used as an alarm-call. A harsh 'cherz' is another common call and in courtship chases it utters a low buzzing 'chiz-chiz'. When there are young in the nest the female utters a very high-pitched 'seep'. The full song is often heard between late August and early December, rarely in mid-July and occasionally between January and late March. It varies greatly in quality but is generally a plaintive, slowly delivered succession of half-a-dozen harsh chuckles and whistles, most notes being variations on a loud 'pee' or 'peeoo', which are sometimes repeated, but more often alternate with the harsh notes. Song is uttered from the ground, bushes, treetops or roofs of buildings. A much quieter subsong of better quality, sung as a continuous warble with the bill closed, has been heard in winter and spring (May to October). Full song does not appear to be important for maintaining established territories, but the following observations show that it can be developed when necessary. One banded male in Stanley sang persistently every day from 3rd to 25th October 1961, from dawn till late evening. Its mate had died at the end of September and it was apparently trying to attract a female. This bird's song was more varied and stronger than any other heard in the Falklands. On Kidney I. in late October 1962 and November 1961 all males around the hut sang each morning from about 0400 till 0600 hours; very little song was heard during the day, although more was heard again in the evening.

FOOD. Mainly worms, fly larvae and pupae, sandhoppers and moth larvae. It also takes several kinds of berries in autumn and winter, particularly pig-vine berries which are abundant and persist till spring. Diddle-dee berries, cultivated currants and strawberries are also eaten. Bread and mutton fat are readily eaten, especially during frosty weather.

HABITAT, STATUS & BREEDING. This common resident is familiar in Stanley and at Camp settlements, where plentiful food and artificial nest-sites in sheds, planted bushes and trees are available. Habitats to which it was probably confined before man colonized the islands, are high rocky crags and slopes where diddle-dee and fern grow thickly, and rock outcrops near the shores of creeks and the sea. It also occurs on tussock-covered islands where rotted kelp heaps are an important source of food. It nests between late August and December, although in a mild winter, nest building may start in mid-July. The nest, which

Southern House Wren on a boulder beach.

Adult male Falkland Thrush in a garden.

is built by the female, is a large structure of dry grass stems and root fibres, sometimes including pieces of string and wool. The deep cup usually has an inner lining of dried mud or dung which itself is lined with fine grass and sometimes also horse hair. Nest-sites vary from sheltered crevices amongst rocks or on top of a bank in long grass or fern to cypress and gorse bushes, or on beams inside peat sheds, wool sheds or any other permanently open buildings. The height of the nest can vary between ground-level and 15–20 ft., but most are between 3 and 7 ft. above ground. On Kidney I., three nests were apparently made entirely of grass; they were sited either at the base of the new growth on top of tussock clumps about 3 ft. above ground or amongst dead stems from two adjacent clumps, which had interlaced to form a platform. It lays 2–3 blue-green eggs, closely marked with brown and purple and usually rears three broods in a season. From five nests watched in Stanley, it was found that the incubation period was 14–16 days from laying the last egg; fledging took 16–18

194

days and the interval to the next nesting, usually in the same nest, was 12–14 days.

About 200 were banded between 1957 and 1963; 91 banded in Stanley and 45 banded on Kidney I. were also colour-banded; the remainder were banded on Carcass, Bleaker and George Is. No long distance recoveries were made and no banded birds from Kidney I. were seen in Stanley, but two birds were once watched flying to the adjacent mainland from Kidney I. One banded as an adult male near Government House, Stanley on 2nd May 1958 was killed by a cat at the west end of Stanley harbour, $2\frac{1}{4}$ miles from the place of banding, $6\frac{1}{2}$ months later. Two colour-banded birds were proved to reach an age of at least 4 years and one of these lived to at least $4\frac{1}{2}$ years. First winter birds banded in autumn were seen often in different parts of Stanley through the winter, but by September most had disappeared and were presumably taking up territories. This species has a high mortality rate in Stanley due to the large number of domestic and feral cats.

DISTRIBUTION ABROAD. The race *T. f. falcklandii* is restricted to the Falkland Is. Another race, *T. f. magellanicus*, inhabits Chile from 27°S and Argentina from 37°S to Tierra del Fuego, Staten I. and Cape Horn.

Falkland/Correndera Pipit

Anthus correndera grayi Bonaparte   A. Cachirla común   C. Bailarín chico
Local names: Skylark, Lark

IDENTIFICATION. Very small. 6″. A slender bird, it is *heavily streaked with buff and dark brown above* and the underparts are yellow-buff streaked with black on breast and flanks. *The tail is brown with conspicuous white sides*, distinguishing it in flight from female and young Black-throated Finches, which have yellow sides to the tail. The bill is thin, fairly short and horn coloured, and the legs are pale pink. A difficult bird to see on the ground, as it runs through grass like a mouse, particularly when near the nest. Flight is jerky over short distances and undulating when flying further.

FOOD. There is little information available, but young in the nest are fed on large numbers of small worms and small moths.

VOICE. The usual call-notes are a short squeaky 'prits' and a higher-pitched hoarse 'princh'. In flight it sometimes gives a triple 'tipitip' call. The song, a pleasant, rather squeaky short phrase of three or four different notes, is heard from mid-August to January and infrequently in March and early April. It is delivered in song-flight when the bird mounts up from the ground rather jerkily to about 100 feet and parachutes down, with the tail held high, while uttering a harsh churring note. Sometimes it stays up for a few minutes singing one song after another, interspersed with parachuting and the churring note; it also sings from the ground.

HABITAT, STATUS & BREEDING. The Pipit is one of the few species preferring the large areas of coarse white grass during the breeding season. It is also found on diddle-dee and grass Camp, on wide sand beaches littered with dead kelp and occasionally on rocky beaches. Common and widespread, it is usually seen singly or in pairs, but small flocks are seen in autumn. Although apparently less numerous in winter in many localities, there is no real evidence of emigration. Possible migratory movements of small parties of 2–4 birds flying high westward, have been observed over Stanley and Kidney I. between mid-March and mid-April. It nests from late September to late December and rears at least two broods in a season. 2–4 eggs are laid, varying in colour from creamy-grey to dirty white, variably spotted and blotched with yellow-brown and purplish-brown with black hairlines near the blunt end. The nest is built of fine grasses sometimes lined with horse hair and is well-hidden in rough grass. Young nestlings can be separated from Black-throated Finches by their dark brown-black down.

DISTRIBUTION ABROAD. The race *A. c. grayi* is confined to the Falkland Is. Other races inhabit South America from Peru and Bolivia (11–20°S) to Chile, and 23°S in Brazil through Paraguay, Uruguay and most of Argentina to Tierra del Fuego.

Long-tailed Meadowlark

Sturnella loyca falklandicus (Leverkuhn)
A. Pecho-colorado grande   C. Loica chilena
Local names: Robin, Starling

IDENTIFICATION. Small. 9½–10″. As the *only red-breasted Falkland passerine*, it is unique, and with its *very heavy pale bill* and loud calls it is quite unmistakable. The *male* in breeding plumage, which is assumed by July, has *brilliant glowing red underparts* from chin to lower breast, *a broad curving white eye-stripe* and dagger-shaped light blue-grey bill. It also has a red spot above and before the eye and red on the carpal joint and leading edge of the wing. All the upper parts including the head are blackish-brown heavily mottled and barred with buff;

Falkland Pipit in thick White grass.

the flanks and belly are mainly black. In autumn and early winter the red is partly obscured by buff tips. The *female* has *an orange-pink throat* and less extensive, paler red on the breast, the eye-stripe is narrower and the bill darker than the male's. The *juvenile* resembles the female but has only *a narrow pink streak in the centre of the underparts* and a shorter bill. In *flight* it can be recognized at a considerable distance by the *pure white underside of the wing*. When on the ground or on a perch it has a typical crouching attitude with the legs almost hidden. It runs with an ungainly action and on occasions moves with powerful bounds. The method of taking flight is unusual; a pair feeding quietly will suddenly shoot up (the male leading) with very rapid wing-beats, almost vertically to about 50 ft., before flying away. (Colour photo: p. 189)

VOICE. The characteristic flight-note is a loud explosive 'cheeoo', which is also used when on the ground. A quieter 'chook' or 'chink' are used mainly when feeding. Song, from both male and female, may be heard during most of the year, but more often in the period August to October. The male has a harsh powerful song (of about seven notes) which falls, rises to a higher note and then falls to a much lower note at the end. It is delivered from the ground, a small hummock, a fence post or even a 50 ft. aerial mast. It is also sometimes delivered in flight and occasionally elaborated and lengthened. The female's song is weaker, more squeaky and shorter than the male's and is often given from the ground while the male sings from a nearby rock or post.

FOOD. The main items of food appear to be insects and worms, which it takes from the soil or basal parts of grass clumps. Moth caterpillars are collected in spring by prodding the bill between grass stems and opening it wide at the same time, thus spreading the stems. Grain left in horse droppings is also eagerly taken, the dung being broken up thoroughly by the same bill actions. It is disliked in some settlements for the habit it has acquired of digging down to potatoes and pecking holes in them.

HABITAT, STATUS & BREEDING. A widely distributed resident, it is most common around settlements and in areas of white grass within half a mile of the seashore. Although pairs are isolated in the breeding season, flocks of up to sixty are formed from January onwards and persist till July. It nests from late August to late November and lays 2–4 blue-white eggs blotched and streaked with purple and black mainly round the large end. Two broods are probably reared in a season. The nest is simply constructed of dry grasses and is well-hidden on the ground in thick white grass, very low tussock-grass or rushes. A nest hidden in dense white grass, containing 3 eggs that were about four days from hatching, had a curved pathway about a yard long leading to it. The female appears to do all building and incubation alone, but both parents feed the young.

DISTRIBUTION ABROAD. The race *S. l. falklandicus* is found only in the Falkland Is. A continental race, is common and widespread in Chile and Argentina from Tierra del Fuego north to 27°S in Chile and 37°S in Argentina. In winter it migrates north to about 23°S in northwest Argentina.

Black-throated Finch

Melanodera m. melanodera (Quoy et Gaimard)
A. Yal garganta negra   C. Yal austral
Local name: Sparrow

IDENTIFICATION. Very small. c6″. An inconspicuous, ground-feeding finch, in which the male and female are quite differently coloured. The male is beautifully patterned with a blue-grey head and mantle, *black throat, black and white facial pattern* and *bright yellow breast*. The flanks are blue-grey and the lower underparts are white. The back and rump are blue-grey variably tinged with olive-green. *The slightly forked tail is dark brown with broad yellow outer edges*, most noticeable at the base, and the wings are also brown with yellow edged flight feathers and yellow lesser coverts. In contrast, the female has drab plumage;

Pair of Black-throated Finches on Stanley Common (male on the left).

the upper parts and head are streaked brown and grey-buff, sometimes tinged with red-brown; it has *a faint buff eye-stripe and dark 'moustache' streak*, and the *flight feathers are dark brown broadly edged with white*. The underparts are buff more or less tinged with yellow and heavily striated with dark brown on either side from neck to flanks. The tail is similar to that of the male, but with less yellow. The *yellow-edged tail* is most noticeable in flight and easily separates the species from the Falkland Pipit. It is distinguished from the Black-chinned Siskin in flight by the absence of a wing-bar. The juvenile resembles the female, while a first-year male, and possibly a winter adult male have the grey and green colour of the head and back partly obscured by red-brown tips. The bill is short and conical, blue-grey in the male and horn-coloured in female and young. The legs are brown. It has a rapid jerky flight and is often seen in small flocks of up to c40 from December to August. The largest flock noted was of about 1,000 near the sand dunes at Yorke Bay on 30th May 1957.

The Yellow-bridled Finch *Melanodera xanthogramma*, (*see* Vagrants list) closely resembles this species, but is somewhat larger, and the male has yellow facial stripes instead of white. The female and juvenile are indistinguishable from those of the Black-throated Finch.

VOICE. The call-note is a very high-pitched short 'si'. Birds feeding amongst thick vegetation and flocks in flight call continually. They produce a distinctive musical sound because the 'si' note is repeated rapidly when each bird moves or a flock is flushed. The male also has a short explosive call, 'spit'; on one occasion it was heard when a male was singing from an outcrop uttering this call frequently between short periods of song. It also uttered a harsh buzzing note while repeatedly chasing a male Black-chinned Siskin from a nearby cypress. The song is a monotonous repetition of two or three phrases 'peeoo, payoo-payoo', the first being slightly higher-pitched than the others. It has been heard between late June and late January, but is most frequent between September and December. Song-perches are mostly low, such as a rock, grass tussock or diddle-dee bush, but fence posts and wires are also used.

FOOD. Feeds mainly on seeds of grasses, sorrel, sand cabbage and diddle-dee berries. It also eats flower spikelets of a Meadow Grass species, seeds of chickweed, and will take bread crumbs. The stomach of a male collected on 28th June 1960 was filled with minute seeds of four kinds. These seeds probably came from round, fleshy fruits such as the Mountain Berry and diddle-dee.

HABITAT, STATUS & BREEDING. A common and widespread resident throughout the Falkland Is. it is found on open grassland close by beaches and to the tops of hills well inland, but it does not occur on islands covered by dense tussock-grass. It nests between mid-September and late December, laying a clutch of 3–4 light blue-grey or grey-green eggs, with purple-brown markings concentrated round the blunt end. It probably rears at least two broods in a season. The nest is constructed of fine grasses and lined with horse hair and down of geese or other feathers, the material being collected by the female, accompanied by the male on each trip. At one nest with 4 eggs the female had no tail, her tail feathers having been used to line the nest. The nest is well-hidden, usually in a white grass tussock; one was found in a crevice beneath a flat stone by a track. Young nestlings may be distinguished from Pipits by their silver-grey down.

DISTRIBUTION ABROAD. The race *M. m. melanodera* is confined to the Falkland Is. *M. m. princetoniana* has a restricted range in southern South America being found only on the Magellanic islands, Tierra del Fuego and to about 49°S in Patagonia.

Rufous-collared Sparrow

Zonotrichia capensis (Latham)   A. Chingolo   C. Chincol

IDENTIFICATION. Minute. c5½″. This fairly long-tailed finch is easily recognized by its *grey head with thick black stripes either side of the crown from bill to nape*. The longer crown feathers are often raised giving the head a peaked appearance. It has a narrow black stripe behind the eye and a *broad chestnut collar across the nape*. The throat is white contrasting with the light grey breast and grey flanks. A small black mark and a continuation of the chestnut collar are conspicuous at the side of the neck. The mantle and wing-coverts are heavily striated with buff and dark brown. The Rufous-collared Sparrow is more slender than the House Sparrow with which it has associated in the Falkland Is.; it is also quicker in its movements and less wary. Its *flight* resembles that of a Pipit, being rather jerky and undulating.

VOICE. The call-note is a short clear 'tseep' repeated frequently. Song, which has been heard occasionally in the Falkland Is., is a short descending phrase.

HABITAT, STATUS & RECORDS. A vagrant that has occurred usually singly, several times in spring and autumn. All were seen at settlements or in Stanley where they fed in gardens with House Sparrows. One was trapped and banded in Stanley on 12th October 1960 being first seen on 11th October. A second bird was seen regularly in one part of Stanley between 11th May and 31st

December 1962. It was caught and banded on 23rd September of that year. It was not possible to assign these to a particular subspecies. Another, seen and photographed at Port Stephens on 9th April 1962 by M. Shaw, was probably a representative of the southern race, *Z. c. australis*, as it lacked the black crown stripes common to the other nine races. It seems probable that the two Stanley birds had assisted passages from Montevideo on R.M.S. *Darwin*, as another definitely travelled from Montevideo to Stanley on R.R.S. *John Biscoe* a few years before 1960. Two appeared on West Point Island in mid-April 1973; by the end of April the chestnut collar was noticeable on both birds. They were still present in mid-August 1973 (D. Davidson, personal communication). It is possible that this species, which is widespread in South America, could colonize the Falkland Is.

DISTRIBUTION ABROAD. Ten races have been described from the tropical and temperate zones of South America. In tropical latitudes they occur mainly in the highlands.

Rufous-collared Sparrow banded in Stanley.

Pair of Black-chinned Siskins on Kidney Island (male on right).

Black-chinned Siskin

Spinus barbatus (Molina)
A. Cabecitanegra de corbata   C. Jilguero común
Local name: Siskin

IDENTIFICATION. Minute. c5″. Smaller size, generally yellow-green plumage, *long broad yellow wing-bar and yellow rump* easily separate this species from the Black-throated Finch. Both sexes are mainly lemon-yellow beneath and dark olive-green above. The dark brown wing shows two yellow bars at rest, but only one in flight. The tail is dark brown with yellow basal sides. *The male has a black crown and chin*, a yellow eye-stripe and is brighter than the female. The juvenile resembles the female. The bill is blackish above and horn-coloured below; the legs and feet are black. It is a very active little bird, with a preference for large bushes, tall tussock-grass and trees. It wanders in small flocks during winter, when they can be detected by their almost continuous rapid twittering.

VOICE. Common call-notes are a shrill rising 'tsooeet' and a House Sparrow-like short 'chit' or 'ti-tip'. The flight-note is a short 'chup'. The song, which is distinctive and carries well, consists of a very hurried mixture of half-a-dozen different notes each repeated 3–5 times together, with a few short trills interspersed. It is frequently sustained almost unbroken for up to ten minutes. Full song has been recorded from May to July and again between October and December.

FOOD. Mainly seeds, which it obtains from diddle-dee berries, garden weeds, and grasses including tussock-grass.

HABITAT, STATUS & BREEDING. Usually found where there is a good growth of bushes around settlements and cliffs. Before 1925 it was uncommon and apparently confined as a breeding species to West Falkland, where it nests in 'box' bushes. It has increased considerably since then and now breeds at some East Falkland settlements and islands, including Port San Carlos, Teal Inlet, Stanley, Kidney I. and Bleaker I. This increase is probably related to the planting of shrubs round settlements, but the species may well have nested on tussock islands in the past and remained undetected. Kidney I. had a breeding population of about ten birds in 1960–62, following a period of about fifteen years since the grass had last been cut for fodder. It is difficult to believe that tussock-covered islands were not formerly occupied by Siskins, when this habitat provides ample food, shelter and nesting sites and moreover was so much more abundant than it is now. It builds a neat, well-formed cup nest of fine grass roots lined with horse hair, wool or grass root fibres, about 4–7 ft. above ground in 'box', barberry, cypress or tussock-grass. 3–5 pinky-white eggs spotted or stippled with red-brown are laid in one clutch. It frequently has up to three broods during the period September to December.

DISTRIBUTION ABROAD. This species is common and widespread in wooded country from Tierra del Fuego and the Magellanic islands to 37°S in the Andes of Argentina and to 27°S in Chile.

House Sparrow

Passer domesticus (Linn.)   A. & C. Gorrión
Local name: English Sparrow

IDENTIFICATION. Very small. c6″. A small, fairly plump, perky bird with dull grey and brown plumage. It is bold and noisy, although at the same time very wary. The male is recognized by its *rich brown nape, dark grey crown, variable black throat patch and whitish cheeks*; the back is brown with black streaks and it shows a short white wing-bar and grey rump in flight. The female and juvenile are alike, dull brown above and dirty white below with a *faint buff eye-stripe*. They can be confused with the female Black-throated Finch but have uniform

Female Black-chinned Siskin on tussock-grass.

underparts and *completely brown tails*. It has a heavy conical bill; the male's bill is black in summer, but otherwise both male and female have yellow-brown bills. The legs are pale brown.

VOICE. It has various harsh squeaky calls and twittering notes. The male has a poor quality song, repeated monotonously, 'chissip, chissip'.

FOOD. Mainly seeds, including grass and weed seeds. It is partial to whole corn (maize) which it can break easily. It also takes insects and much other small food including caterpillars from grass in spring and early summer, bread-crumbs and grain scattered for domestic fowls.

HABITAT, STATUS & BREEDING. A self-introduced species in the Falkland Is., it has become numerous only in Stanley, due to its inability to adapt itself to an environment away from man and his settlements. First recorded in

Stanley in 1919 when about twenty arrived on one or more whaling vessels from Montevideo. From Stanley it has spread to Teal Inlet, Fitzroy, Green Patch and Darwin, although dates of colonization at these settlements are not known. In late October 1959, three pairs arrived at Carcass I. and remained; nearby West Point I. also has a small colony of about half-a-dozen dating from 1958–59. Both colonies were still in existence in late 1965. They are both closely attached to the settlement buildings and gardens. How this species colonized these two islands, both over 100 miles from Stanley, is not known. As it is unrecorded on the West Falkland mainland, these birds possibly travelled round from Stanley on the local mail and cargo vessel or may have been drifted from the coast of Argentina. It breeds colonially, building a large untidy nest of grasses under roofs or in any available hole high up on a building. On Carcass I. the whole colony nests socially in one large cypress tree. The main season is probably from September onwards, but little information is available. Clutch size in the Falkland Is. is not known, but in England is 3–5, occasionally 6 or 7. The eggs are greyish-white finely spotted with brown and grey.

DISTRIBUTION ABROAD. Originally confined to Europe, North Africa and Asia, where it is very widely distributed. Now introduced and numerous in North and South America, Australia and New Zealand, it is a sedentary species that rarely migrates.

ABOVE Dense white grass and diddle-dee on Stanley Common (*see p.* 22). BELOW Misery Valley, West Point I., looking towards West Falkland mainland with Saunders I. in distance. Replanted tussock-grass in the foreground (*see p.* 30).

Vagrants and Lost Breeding Species

Near Felton Stream, west of Stanley (*see p.* 16).

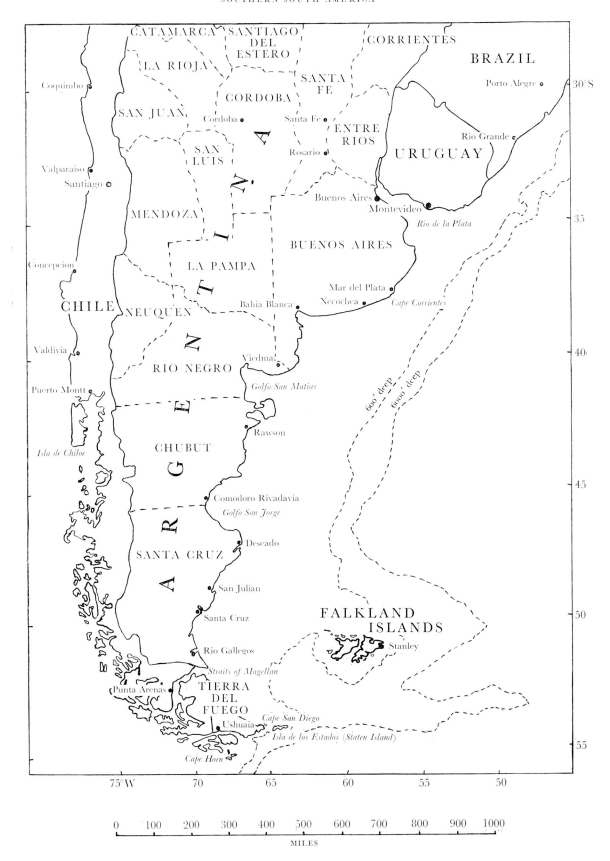

Coquimbo

CATAMARCA SANTIAGO DEL ESTERO

CORRIENTES

BRAZIL

Porto Alegre

30° S

LA RIOJA

SANTA FE

SAN JUAN

CORDOBA

Cordoba

Santa Fe

Rio Grande

ENTRE RIOS

Valparaiso

SAN LUIS

Rosario

URUGUAY

Santiago

A R G E N T I N A

Buenos Aires

Montevideo

MENDOZA

Rio de la Plata

35

BUENOS AIRES

Concepcion

LA PAMPA

Mar del Plata

CHILE

NEUQUEN

Bahia Blanca

Necochea

Cape Corrientes

Valdivia

RIO NEGRO

Viedma

40

Golfo San Matias

600' deep

6000' deep

Puerto Montt

Isla de Chiloe

Rawson

CHUBUT

45

Comodoro Rivadavia

Golfo San Jorge

Deseado

SANTA CRUZ

San Julian

50

Santa Cruz

FALKLAND ISLANDS

Rio Gallegos

Straits of Magellan

Stanley

Punta Arenas

TIERRA DEL FUEGO

Ushuaia

Cape San Diego

Isla de los Estados (Staten Island)

55

Cape Horn

75° W   70   65   60   55   50

0   100   200   300   400   500   600   700   800   900   1000

MILES

Vagrants and Lost Breeding Species

This annotated list includes published and unpublished records of accidental visitors from South America and antarctic regions. A few species are discussed that have not been observed in recent years, although it is possible that some may still breed in the Falkland Islands. Several species are included on the strength of sight-records alone. It was considered useful to mention the species that have probably occurred because they may appear in the future.

Ranges of all species have been given to indicate the distances they may have travelled in order to reach the Falkland Islands. This information was obtained from the following works: *Birds of the Ocean* (Alexander, 1955), *Las Aves de Chile* (Goodall, Johnson & Philippi, 1951 & 1957), *A Guide to the Birds of South America* (Meyer de Schaunsee, 1971), *Oceanic Birds of South America* (Murphy, 1936), *Las Aves Argentinas* (Olrog, 1959), *Lista Sistematica de las Aves Argentinas* (Zotta, 1944).

In this list, the term 'winter' means 'Southern winter' (roughly from April to September) unless stated otherwise.

Emperor Penguin

Aptenodytes forsteri G. R. Gray

Two records; an adult stayed on Pebble I. for five days in late April 1936 and a 'probable immature' was seen in or near Foul Bay, East Falkland in early April 1954. Both birds were photographed (Hamilton 1954). *Range:* Circumpolar on shores of the antarctic continent. In summer migrates northward (in West Antarctica) along both coasts of the Antarctic Peninsula to South Shetlands and occasionally to South Orkneys. It has also occurred at Tierra del Fuego and Kerguelen I.

Adelie Penguin

Pygoscelis adeliae (Hombron & Jacquinot)

One was seen and photographed by A. Carey at the head of Berkeley Sound early in December 1961. *Range:* Circumpolar round the antarctic continent, also breeding north to the South Shetlands, South Orkneys and South Sandwich Is. It winters on free pack-ice and is rarely noted north of 60°S.

Chinstrap Penguin

Pygoscelis antarctica (Forster)

One seen in Stanley harbour in June 1915 (Bennett 1926); one seen at Port Stephens on 23rd January 1916 (Brooks 1917); one caught on Bleaker I. on 23rd March 1959, was leg-banded with a Falkland Islands Dependencies Survey (now British Antarctic Survey) band and released on 2nd April 1959. *Range:* Almost confined to West Antarctica (3°E–90°W), it breeds at the South Shetlands, South Sandwich and South Orkney Is. and in small numbers at other places, including South Georgia, Peter and Macquarie Is. It is pelagic in winter.

Erect-crested Penguin

Eudyptes sclateri Buller

One was seen at the same Rockhopper Penguin rookery on West Point I. each year from November 1961 to January 1967. It was thought at first to be a Macaroni Penguin, but was identified as this species in November 1964. R. B. Napier photographed the bird and identification was confirmed by Dr. W. J. L. Sladen of the United States Antarctic Research Program, Bird-Banding Program, Baltimore. *Range:* Breeds at Auckland, Antipodes & Bounty Is. and in very small numbers at Campbell I., all south of New Zealand. Occasionally wanders north to New Zealand and southern Australia.

Great Grebe

Podiceps major Boddaert

One damaged and decaying male was found at San Carlos in the spring of 1941 (Cawkell & Hamilton 1961); another was seen by Mr. and Mrs. C. Bertrand in the harbour at Carcass I. for several days in February 1966. One stayed in the harbour at West Point I. for nearly two months after 16th January 1967. *Range:* From 30°S in Chile, Brazil, Paraguay and Uruguay, through Argentina to Tierra del Fuego, but absent from the Andes. Also on the coast of Peru between 5° and 10°S.

Yellow-nosed Albatross

Diomedea chlororhynchos Gmelin

R. H. Beck saw this species a number of times near the Falklands in September 1915 (Murphy 1936) but there are no recent records. It is not easily distinguished from the Grey-headed Albatross at sea. *Range:* Breeds at Tristan da Cunha, Gough and St. Paul Is. in the temperate South Atlantic and Indian Oceans. It occurs mostly between 30° and 50°S in all southern oceans.

Antarctic Petrel

Thalassoica antarctica (Gmelin)

One bird, almost certainly of this species, was flushed near the shore of Port Harriet, south of Stanley, on 28th February 1957. E. M. P. Salmon found one freshly dead near Eliza Cove on 23rd September 1959. It was later skinned and the skin is now in the British Museum. *Range:* Breeds on the coasts of the antarctic continent; the flight range is circumpolar in antarctic waters usually where pack-ice is present; it rarely reaches 50°S, but has occurred among southern Magellanic islands.

White-headed Petrel

Pterodroma lessonii (Garnot)

Three were reported flying near the north coast of East Falkland on 23rd August 1925 (Bennett 1931). One bird, possibly of this species, was seen about 300 miles north of the Falkland Is. on 21st December 1956. Bennett stated in his 1926 List that the Falkland Is. were the type-locality, but it appears that Garnot's type-specimen did *not* come from the Falkland Is. According to Dabbene (*Hornero*, Feb. 1923, p. 16) Garnot's original description of this species' type-locality was '. . . dans les parages du Cap Horn et de la mer Pacifique, par 52° de lat. et 85° de long'. Dabbene continued, '—Habit. subst. Falkland Isl. Seas, aut. Mathews, "A List of the Birds of Australia", p. 37; 1913'. Mathews apparently reversed Garnot's '85°de long.' to 58° longitude (W), thereby implying that the bird was obtained in Falkland seas. *Range:* Breeds at Kerguelen I. and at Auckland, Antipodes and Macquarie Is. south of New Zealand. Occurs in southern oceans between about 60° and 33°S, but is uncommon in the western South Atlantic.

Soft-plumaged Petrel

Pterodroma mollis (Gould)

One dead specimen was found at Teal Inlet in late March 1945 (Hamilton 1945). *Range:* Breeds at Tristan da Cunha, Gough and St. Paul Is.; another race breeds at Madeira and the Cape Verde Is. The southern race occurs commonly in the South Atlantic and Indian Oceans between 25° and 50°S and is regularly observed on the journey between Stanley and Montevideo.

Snow Petrel

Pagodroma nivea (Forster)

Bennett (1926) stated that this was an occasional winter visitor, but there are no recent records. *Range:* Breeds at the South Shetlands, South Orkneys, South Georgia and on the antarctic continent. It is almost confined to antarctic waters with bergs or pack ice and very rarely reaches 50°S.

Broad-billed Prion

Pachyptila forsteri (Latham)

One struck Cape Pembroke Light in August 1912 (Bennett 1926); the second was found dead on West Falkland in July 1940 (C. & H. 1961); a third specimen was found freshly dead at Eliza Cove near Stanley on 3rd September 1963, and was later skinned by D. Davidson. *Range:* Breeds at Tristan da Cunha and Gough Is. and at islands around New Zealand including the Chathams and Auckland Is. Its flight range is in the warmer northern parts of sub-antarctic waters.

Dove Prion

Pachyptila desolata (Gmelin)

Partly eaten remains of one bird were found on the shore at Christina Bay near Stanley on 11th January 1961. They included the complete upper mandible, from which it was identified. *Range:* Breeds at Cape Denison on the antarctic continent and at antarctic and sub-antarctic islands of South Georgia, South Orkneys, Heard, Kerguelen, Auckland and Macquarie. Its flight range is circumpolar between about 35° and 65°S, though it has reached 25°S off the Chilean coast and 24°S off the Brazilian coast.

Black-bellied Storm-Petrel

Fregetta tropica (Gould)

This is probably a migrant visitor to Falkland seas, but there are no documented records (see Cawkell 1960). *Range:* Breeds at the South Shetlands, South Orkneys, South Georgia, Bouvet, Crozets, Kerguelen and some sub-antarctic islands south of New Zealand. It ranges north to the tropics and occasionally crosses the Equator.

Magellan Diving Petrel

Pelecanoides magellani (Mathews)

Two specimens were recently found in the British Museum by W. R. P. Bourne, who supplied the following information. 'The specimens were dated 1888 "Falkland Is." and 29th March 1930; the latter specimen struck Cape Pembroke Light and was collected by J. E. Hamilton.' Apart from these skins, the species is unknown in the Falkland Islands. It may have occurred as a vagrant, but it could breed on outlying tussock islands, because Diving Petrels are strictly nocturnal and very difficult to observe at their breeding-grounds. *Range:* Coasts of southern Chile and Argentina from 42°S and 48°S respectively, to Cape Horn.

Brown Booby

Sula leucogaster (Boddaert)

One was seen by Garnot about 1820 (Bennett 1926), but there are no recent records. *Range:* Common in tropical and sub-tropical seas; several races breed on islands and coasts in the tropical Atlantic, Indian and Pacific Oceans.

Red-legged Cormorant

Phalacrocorax gaimardi (Lesson et Garnot)

One was seen near West Point I. by R. B. Napier in about January 1950 (date uncertain). Another was seen in West Point I. harbour by R. B. Napier in late April and May 1965, possibly also in September 1965. *Range:* Pacific coast of South America from 9°S in Peru to 43°S, less frequently to 53°S; also on the coast of Argentina only at Puerto Deseado (47°S).

Snowy Egret

Egretta thula (Molina)

One was found dead below Cape Pembroke Light on the night of 3rd May 1957. The body was partly eaten by feral cats, but the remains were later identified at the British Museum. The meteorological situation at the time when this bird occurred in the Falkland Is. is shown on page 34. On examination of weather charts for June 1960, after the Striated Heron and Purple Gallinule had been recorded, a remarkably similar situation was found to have been prevailing in both years. In early May 1957 and mid-June 1960 both situations were dominated by a travelling anticyclone. These high pressure areas intensified over Buenos Aires province and then drifted southeast over the South Atlantic. In both cases they brought unusually strong northerly winds which covered the whole track between eastern Argentina and the Falkland Islands. *Range:* Breeds from the southern United States through Central and South America to about 40°S in Chile and Argentina.

Striated Heron

Butorides striatus (Linn.)

One badly damaged specimen was found on Carcass I. in June 1960 by C. and K. Bertrand; it was identified at the British Museum. (See weather chart in *Introduction* and discussion under the previous species.) *Range:* Africa, Asia, Australia and South America, mostly in tropical and lower temperate regions to 36°S.

Maguari Stork

Euxenura maguari (Molina)

A description was received from Mrs. D. Goodwin of a very large white bird, with black either side of the back and probably a black tail. It had long pink legs, a longish pink bill and golden patches either side of the bill. It landed in a paddock at Horseshoe Bay on 24th August 1961, and was almost certainly a bird of this species. *Range:* Throughout most of South America from the Guianas to 42°S in Argentina, but it is only a rare visitor to 52°S in Chile.

Roseate Spoonbill

Ajaia ajaja (Linn.)

One was found dead near Stanley in 1922 (Bennett 1926); another found long dead at Rolon Cove, near Stanley, in the winter of 1953, may have been one of a small flock once reported to have been trapped in ice there (C. and H. 1961); one was found dead near Port San Carlos on 31st May 1962 and sent to Stanley by N. K. Cameron. *Range:* Breeds from the southern United States throughout most of eastern South America to about 38°S in Argentina. It also occurs further south to about 52°S in Argentina and rarely in central Chile (33°S).

Chilean Flamingo

Phoenicopterus chilensis Molina

One was present for some months from autumn 1910 till the following spring near Hope Harbour, West Falkland. Another, possibly the same bird, was seen in a small lagoon at the head of Byron Sound in February 1911 (Vallentin 1924); one was obtained on 28th June 1924 (no locality given) (Bennett 1926); one was seen in a pond near Fitzroy in 1932 by J. E. Hamilton (C. and H. 1961). *Range:* Occurs throughout southern South America from 20°S in Chile and in Bolivia, southern Brazil, and all Argentina to about 55°S.

White-cheeked/Bahama Pintail

Anas bahamensis Vieillot

Bennett (1926) stated that this was an accidental visitor, but no documented records were cited. *Range:* Breeds in the Guianas, Venezuela, south and east Brazil, Paraguay, Uruguay and eastern Bolivia and is scarce in northern Argentina to about 40°S. It occurs in northern and central Chile (18–38°S) during periods of prolonged drought in its breeding areas.

Red Shoveler

Anas platalea Vieillot

Bennett (1926) stated that this species was also an accidental visitor, but no records were cited. Hamilton saw some females or immatures on Swan Pond, Cape Dolphin, but no date is given (C. & H. 1961). *Range:* Breeds from southern Peru, Bolivia, southern Brazil and Uruguay throughout most of Argentina (23–53°S) and Chile (33–53°S), but it is less common south of 43°S.

Rosy-billed Pochard

Netta peposaca (Vieillot)

Five specimens were obtained from a flock of about thirty seen in 1920, but the locality was not stated (Bennett 1926). One male was seen on Sedge I. early in September 1966 and a pair were seen on Carcass I. on 18th and 19th September 1966. There was a period of exceptionally strong westerly winds during the second week of September. *Range:* Breeds in Paraguay, Uruguay, southern Brazil, central Chile (28–42°S, scarce) and Argentina (30–42°S). In winter it occurs in northern Argentina (24–30°S).

Lake Duck

Oxyura vittata (Philippi)

'A number' were seen in the Falkland Islands in 1916–17 during a drought in Argentina, but no localities were stated (Bennett 1926). None have been recorded since. *Range:* Southern Brazil, Paraguay, Uruguay, Chile (28–42°S) and Argentina (22–55°S), but not found in the Andes.

Cinereous Harrier

Circus cinereus Vieillot

Darwin saw this species during his visits in 1833–34, observing that it was very tame for a bird of prey and that it fed on molluscs, insects and small quadrupeds. The latter were presumably introduced rabbits, rats or mice. He also watched one feeding from the carcass of a cow. Abbott (1860, in Crawshay 1907) stated that it was resident throughout the year but far from plentiful. He remarked that it was very bold; young birds often followed him when out rabbit-hunting but he did not see one kill a rabbit. By 1926 Bennett classified it as an accidental visitor, with the brief remark that 'it may have been common in former days, possibly even bred'. To complete the record of this species in the Falkland Is. to date, Hamilton had a report suggesting breeding in the last thirty-five years (C. & H. 1961), one was seen on West Point I. in mid-February

1973, and another probably an immature male, on West Point I. on 12th August 1973 (D. Davidson).

The loss of this beautiful bird from the islands' avifauna is very regrettable and can probably be attributed to two main factors; its innate indifference to man made it an easy target for men with guns, and its habit of nesting on open grassland exposed eggs and young to the danger of trampling from the rapidly increasing herds of cattle in the mid-19th century. The practice of grass-burning, which came later when sheep-farming was well established, probably finished it as a breeding species. *Range:* Most of western and southern South America from Colombia, southeastern Brazil, Peru and eastern Bolivia through Chile (27–55°S) and Argentina to Tierra del Fuego.

Chimango Caracara

Milvago chimango (Vieillot)

One long-dead specimen was found on West Falkland in the 1940's (C. & H. 1961). G. Stewart described a bird, almost certainly of this species, which he saw at Beaver I. in early June 1960 (personal communication). Apart from these two records, this species is unknown in the Falkland Is. H. K. Swann (1924–30) reproduced notes written by A. G. Bennett on its breeding habits, which stated that it bred in the Falkland Is., but only on remote uninhabited islands. The nest, placed in a tuft of 'junco' [rush], from pieces of which it was constructed, was lined with wool and hair. Yet Bennett did not mention it in his 1926 List. No instances of breeding have been noted or published, so it can only be classed as an accidental visitor from South America. *Range:* Common in southern South America from Bolivia, Paraguay, and southeastern Brazil (20–28°S), through Uruguay, Argentina and Chile between 28° and 56°S. The southern (37–56°S) populations are separated as the race *M. c. temucoensis* which is darker than the typical race.

Speckled Crake

Coturnicops notata (Gould)

One was caught on the banks of a small stream near Stanley on 25th April 1921 (Bennett 1926). *Range:* Occurs in parts of Venezuela, Guyana, Colombia and southeastern Brazil, and between 30° and 42°S in Uruguay and Argentina.

Purple Gallinule

Porphyrula martinica (Linn.)

The remains of one were found by the Mile Pond, south of Stanley on 23rd September 1934 (Bennett 1935); a second specimen, a first year bird (identity and age confirmed by the British Museum, Natural History) was caught by a cat at Port Louis in mid-June 1960 (see notes on the meteorological situation under Snowy Egret). *Range:* Southern United States, Central America and South America from the Guianas and Venezuela through Peru, Bolivia and southern Brazil, Uruguay, Chile and northern Argentina to about 35°S.

White-winged Coot

Fulica leucoptera Vieillot

One coot seen at Goose Green settlement by M. Shaw between late February and early March 1960 was apparently of this species. Notes received on the colour of bill and frontal shield suggested that it was neither a Red-gartered nor a Red-fronted Coot. *Range:* Breeds from eastern Bolivia, southeastern Brazil, Paraguay and Uruguay throughout Chile (18–55°S) and all Argentina (23–53°S) except the Andean plateau.

Red-fronted Coot

Fulica rufifrons Philippi & Landbeck

Several were seen in 1915 and one was obtained on 9th October. In November 1924 another was alive in captivity in Stanley (Bennett 1926). Although Bennett considered that it might breed occasionally, there have been none recorded since 1924. *Range:* Found in Paraguay (rarely), southeastern Brazil, Uruguay, all Argentina except the Andes (23–53°S) and in central Chile (27–38°S), although it probably also occurs further south in Chile.

Tawny-throated Dotterel

Oreopholus ruficollis (Wagler)

Bennett (1926) considered that this species might breed in the Falkland Is. and it was represented by a specimen of local origin in the old Stanley Museum. However there were no documented records until two were seen by W. May on West Point I. on 28th August 1961. One bird was standing close to another that lay dead on the hillside, presumably killed by a feral cat. The dead bird was sent to Stanley for identification. None have been seen since and it appears that the species is only an accidental visitor at times of migration. *Range*: Breeds throughout the Andean regions of Chile, Argentina and Bolivia from about 18°S to Tierra del Fuego. It occurs in eastern Argentina, Uruguay, Peru and Ecuador in winter.

Magellanic Plover

Pluvianellus socialis G. R. Gray

A description was received from C. A. J. Nelson of a plover that arrived at Salvador settlement during a storm in late March 1959 and survived, living in and near the cowshed, until early June 1959. It was almost certainly a bird of this species and immature, because the legs were yellow instead of carmine, as they are in the adult. *Range:* Breeds only in northern Tierra del Fuego and the Magellanic islands. In winter it occurs north to about 45°S in Argentina.

Lesser Yellowlegs

Tringa flavipes (Gmelin)

One was shot near Stanley on 5th May 1924 (Bennett 1926). *Range:* Breeds in Canada from about 50–70°N and migrates south to spend the northern winter in Chile, Paraguay, Uruguay and Argentina between about 18° and 55°S.

Baird's Sandpiper

Calidris bairdii (Coues)

One was noted about 1920, presumably by Bennett, and reported in *Ibis*, April 1921, p. 312. One was seen on 2nd January 1955 at Hearnden Water, near Stanley, in company with some White-rumped Sandpipers (C. & H. 1961). *Range:* Breeds in arctic North America from western Alaska to Baffin Land and south to about 64°N. Migrates south and in the northern winter occurs in large flocks from about 18–40°S in Chile and throughout Argentina to Tierra del Fuego (55°S).

Upland Plover

Bartramia longicauda (Bechstein)

One was found exhausted on 29th May 1938 near Stanley, and another bird, thought by Bennett (1938) to be of the same species, was seen being carried off by a cat. One was reported near the Power Station at Stanley on 26th October 1961 by J. Blyth. It was later watched on the football field nearby, feeding avidly on worms and caterpillars which it took from rough grass. It displayed (with bill open and tail fanned and depressed slightly) at several Falkland Thrushes hopping inquisitively nearby. When last seen on this field on 31st October, it still appeared in good condition. *Range:* Breeds from the central United States (39°N) to northwestern Alaska (70°N) and migrates through North and Central America to southern Brazil and Argentina to about 42°S, where it occurs in its non-breeding season, the southern summer.

Whimbrel

Numenius phaeopus hudsonicus Latham

A description was received from Mrs. K. Bertrand of a large snipe-coloured bird with long dark legs, long down-curved bill and dark stripe above the eye, that was seen near a pond on Carcass I. on 7th December 1962. It was probably this species. *Range:* Breeds on arctic coasts of North America and migrates south to spend the northern winter on the west coast of Central and South America (to 45°S in Chile) and on the east coast regularly to Bahia (13°S) and accidentally as far as Tierra del Fuego (55°S).

Eskimo Curlew

Numenius borealis (J. R. Forster)

This species has not been recorded with any certainty in the past fifty years. *Range:* Formerly bred in northern Canada and Alaska and migrated to central Argentina and southern Brazil for the northern winter, but it is now almost extinct due to excessive shooting of migrating flocks.

Hudsonian Godwit

Limosa haemastica (Linn.)

Several specimens were obtained in the Falkland Islands during the 19th century by Captain Abbott, Darwin, Admiral Fitzroy and Captain Pack. There have been no further records since Captain Abbott saw a flock at Mare Harbour in May 1860. *Range:* Breeds in arctic North America and migrates to the Atlantic coast and inland South America from about 18–55°S for the northern winter. It is seen occasionally on the Pacific coast. It was formerly abundant but suffered like the Eskimo Curlew from shooting of migrating flocks. Its numbers have apparently increased in recent years.

Red Phalarope

Phalaropus fulicarius (Linn.)

This species is said to have occurred in the latitude of the Falkland Is., presumably during the northern winter when it is leading a pelagic life in South American waters, but no specimens are known (Murphy 1936). *Range:* Breeds in arctic North America, arctic Europe and Asia, south to about 55°N. North American birds spend the northern winter at sea off the Pacific coast of South America to about 43°S off Chile. It occurs accidentally in Paraguay and Argentina.

Wilson's Phalarope

Steganopus tricolor (Vieillot)

One specimen from the University College Museum, Dundee, that was said to have originated from the Falkland Is., was exhibited in 1895 by P. L. Sclater (Sclater 1895). There are no other records. *Range:* Breeds in central and western North America and migrates to southern South America in the northern winter where it occurs more inland than on the sea. It reaches about 42°S in Argentina and occurs rarely in northern Chile (18°S).

White-bellied Seedsnipe

Attagis malouinus (Boddaert)

Apart from the type-specimen named in 1783 and a single specimen shot on the beach at Mare Harbour early in October 1859 by Captain Abbott, there are no other records. It may have been a breeding species a century ago that was soon exterminated in the Falkland Is. by a combination of over-grazing and grass-burning. *Range:* Breeds only on the high moorland and mountains of southern Chile (from 50°S) and Argentina from about 40°S to the islands south of Tierra del Fuego and Staten I.

Grey Gull

Larus modestus Tschudi

One was observed at Stanley for three weeks in August 1953; it associated with

Kelp and Dolphin Gulls (C. & H. 1961). *Range:* Breeds only in northern Chile and Peru on high Andean deserts. It occurs on the Pacific coast from 5° to 30°S commonly, and is occasionally seen as far as 47°S. It has not been recorded in Argentina.

Common Tern

Sterna hirundo Linn.

One specimen was taken at Cape Pembroke on 15th September 1945; the skin is now in the British Museum (C. & H. 1961). This species may occur regularly in Falkland seas during the southern summer (October–March). *Range:* Breeds in Europe, North America and the Caribbean. North American breeding birds spend the northern winter on both coasts of South America as far as the Magellan Straits (53°S).

Chilean Pigeon

Columba araucana Lesson

One adult male in poor condition was shot at Teal Inlet on 19th September 1941 (Hamilton 1950). *Range:* Breeds in the forests of central and southern Chile (28–47°S) and in the Andean region of southern Argentina (36–52°S).

Burrowing Parrot

Cyanoliseus patagonus (Vieillot)

One large parrot-like bird seen on New I. on 1st May 1959 by J. Davis and others, was probably of this species. It flew overhead calling and was later seen eating diddle-dee berries. *Range:* Three races breed in central Chile (30–40°S), northwestern Argentina (25–35°S) and central Argentina (35–42°S).

Austral Parakeet

Enicognathus ferrugineus P. L. S. Muller

During the week 14th–21st June 1957 there was apparently an 'invasion' of a species of parakeet in the Falkland Is. Many were seen at various places, including New, Beaver and West Point Is. (26 at the latter island), Fox Bay, Speedwell I. and at Chartres where about 60 were counted on one roof by W. Carlisle. On 8th April 1959 about 10 were seen at Fox Bay East by Mrs. D. B. Marshall; 2

were seen on Barren I. on 22nd April and one was seen in Stanley during the same week (J. Booth, personal communication). No specimens were collected, but several descriptions received suggest that the parakeets were of this species. *Range:* The race *E. f. f.* occurs only in Tierra del Fuego and the Magellanic region of Chile; a smaller race, *E. f. minor* is found in the Andean region of southern Argentina between 40° and 52°S and in Chile between 35° and 47°S.

Dark-billed Cuckoo

Coccyzus melacoryphus Dabbene

One male was caught in Government House garden in Stanley on 7th April 1937, but died soon afterwards. It was thought to have been in the area for three weeks (Bennett 1937). *Range:* Most of South America from the Guianas and Venezuela southwards to about 36°S in Argentina, but absent from Chile.

Ashy-tailed Swift

Chaetura andrei meridionalis Hellmayr

One was found mummified and in perfect condition at the Naval Wireless Station west of Stanley, by B. Withers on 1st March 1959. It had apparently entered an unused shed through a partly open window and been unable to escape. The specimen was identified from a description by Sr. R. Plotnick of the Instituto Patologia Vegetal, Jose C. Paz, F.C.G.S.M., Argentina. *Range:* Surinam, Venezuela and northern Colombia, eastern and southern Brazil from 5°S, Paraguay and northern Argentina to 30°S. This species therefore does not normally occur within 1,500 miles of the Falkland Is.

Green-backed Firecrown

Sephanoides sephanoides (Lesson & Garnot)

One male was caught on West Falkland, probably at Fox Bay, between 1910 and 1912 (M. White, personal communication; skin seen by D. Davidson). One was picked up dead, having apparently hit a telegraph wire, at Fox Bay East in late October 1930 (Bennett 1931). One 'Hummingbird' possibly of this species, was caught and eaten by the cat at Government House, Stanley in 1952 (Cawkell, unpublished ms.). One female was caught in the greenhouse at Government House on 28th March 1963 by P. Peck. It died the following day and was later skinned. This bird weighed 4·25 gms. and had survived a journey of 450 miles without food. *Range:* Breeds over a wide range in Chile from about 28°S to 55°S in Tierra del Fuego and from about 6,000 feet in the Andes to sea-level. In Argentina it breeds only in the Andean regions from 32°S to 55°S. In winter it occurs also in eastern parts of Argentina and further north (to 27°S) in Chile, as well as making vertical migrations from Andean regions to lower ground.

Thorn-tailed Rayadito

Aphrastura spinicauda (Gmelin)

One adult specimen from the Falkland Is. was presented to the British Museum by the Admiralty in the 19th century (Sclater *et al* B.M.C. Vol. XV, p. 30). A report received in 1963 from C. Bertrand suggested that unfamiliar small birds seen on Sea Lion Easterly in the 1930s were actually this species. This island has never been stocked, is uninhabited and remote from permanently inhabited islands. It is quite possible that this species still exists there as the habitat would appear to be perfectly suitable. Reynolds (1935) describes how it is at home on treeless Barnevelt I. (east of Cape Horn) where 'it has found an excellent substitute for trees in the huge groves of tussock grass'. *Range:* Common in the forests of southern Chile (from 30°S) and Argentina (from 37°S) to Tierra del Fuego, Staten I. and the Magellanic islands (56°S).

Austral Canastero

Asthenes anthoides (King)

Darwin collected an adult specimen in the Falkland Is. in 1833 or 1834, which is now in the British Museum (Sclater *et al* B.M.C. Vol. XV, p. 70). This species may have occurred as a vagrant from Tierra del Fuego, but there is a distinct possibility that it formerly bred in the Falkland Is. *Range:* Found in South America from Peru and Bolivia to Tierra del Fuego. It is most common in the northern part of its Chilean range (39–42°S) and occurs in pastures and foothills of the Andes to about 3,500 feet. In winter southern birds migrate north in Chile to about 32°S.

Andean Tapaculo

Scytalopus magellanicus (Gmelin)

Darwin collected one juvenile specimen in the Falkland Is. in 1833 or 1834

(Sclater *et al* B.M.C. Vol. XV, p. 338–9). Bennett believed that he saw one near Stanley in 1916 (Bennett 1926). Although Darwin collected only one specimen, it appears from his notes that he saw others and that it was a breeding species. He stated that, 'It has found its way over to the Falkland Is., where, instead of inhabiting forests, it frequents the coarse herbage and low bushes, which in most parts conceal the peaty surface of that island.' (Gould & Darwin 1838–41). Low bushes (e.g. Fachine) *were* a feature of the vegetation before sheep were introduced in numbers about fifteen years later. Darwin also remarked that it could be mistaken for a wren and was difficult to observe, which may partly account for the fact that it was not seen or recognized by later observers. But it is probable that it had practically disappeared by the end of the 19th century and no ornithologist was present to notice its decrease or disappearance.

Reynolds (1932) observed this species on Snipe I. in the Beagle Channel south of Tierra del Fuego where it occupied a habitat that he described as a 'pseudo-Falkland Island setting'. The island, which lacked trees, had instead a surprisingly luxuriant flora which included *Berberis*, *Veronica* and tussock-grass. This information and Darwin's notes support the possibility that this species of tapaculo could still survive on uninhabited outer islands of the Falklands. *Range:* The southern race *S. m. m.* is common in southern Chile and southern Argentina (Andean region only) from about 37°S to Tierra del Fuego and Cape Horn. Other races occur from Venezuela, Colombia and Bolivia to western Argentina.

Black-billed Shrike-tyrant

Agriornis montana leucura Gould

R. B. Napier saw a large Ground-tyrant ('twice the size of the Dark-faced Ground-tyrant, with a heavy bill') on West Point I. on 8th December 1963. He considered it was almost certainly this species and race, after checking his notes against descriptions of several similar species in 'Las Aves de Chile'. *Range:* Andes of southeastern Colombia, Ecuador, Peru and Bolivia to 48°S in Argentina and to 52°S in Chile.

Fire-eyed Diucon

Pyrope pyrope (Kittlitz)

Vallentin is said to have seen one between 1898 and 1911 (Bennett 1926). One

Fire-eyed Diucon; a rare vagrant from South America.

was present at the west end of Stanley harbour between late April and mid-July 1961. It was closely observed and photographed on 10th July; full field-notes were taken and comparisons made with a Dark-faced Ground-tyrant nearby. It fed by picking up small insects from flooded grass (sometimes after hovering about two feet above the ground) and carrying them back to a fence-post. Larvae of a type of caddis-fly were seen being eaten whole or being broken from the case by banging it on the fence-post. *Range:* Common in the valleys and foothills of the Andes to 4,500 ft. in Chile from 32–55°S. Also found in the Argentine Andes from 36–55°S. In winter migrates north to about 27°S in Chile.

White-browed Ground-tyrant

Muscisaxicola albilora Lafresnaye

H. Bennett found one injured in Stanley on 25th February 1949 (C. & H. 1961). *Range:* Andean regions of southern South America between about 4,500 and 7,500 ft. from 32°S in Chile and 36°S in Argentina to 53°S. Migrates north in winter to Peru, Bolivia and Ecuador (0–23°S).

Rufous-backed Negrito

Lessonia rufa (Gmelin)

One male was seen on West Point I. on 28th September 1963 by R. B. Napier. It was easily recognized by its all-dark plumage apart from a chestnut back. *Range:* Widely distributed from the coast to 6,000 ft., particularly near water or marshy ground, from 18°S in Chile and 23°S in Argentina to 55°S, including Staten I. Southern birds migrate north to extreme southeastern Brazil, Paraguay and Uruguay.

Fork-tailed Flycatcher

Muscivora tyrannus (Linn.)

One was found dead at Saunders I. in December 1930 (Kinnear 1931). One was present at West Point I. for about a week during October 1966 (R. B. Napier). One was seen on New I. in January 1972 (Pettingill, 1973). *Range:* Most of South America east of the Andes, from the Guianas and eastern Brazil through Bolivia, Paraguay and Uruguay to about 40°S in Argentina. This is a highly migratory species.

Great Kiskadee

Pitangus sulphuratus Lafresnaye

One was present at Port Stephens settlement from 21st March to 8th April 1962, where it was seen and identified by M. Shaw. It associated with a party of Falkland Thrushes, but was very shy and left them whenever disturbed. It apparently dwelt in a small *Macrocarpa* wood behind the house, where it was seen trying to catch flies. *Range:* Central South America east of the Andes from Bolivia and southern Brazil through Paraguay and Uruguay to about 39°S in northern Argentina. It is apparently not migratory.

White-crested Elaenia

Elaenia albiceps chilensis Hellmayr

One specimen was obtained in Stanley on 15th December 1934 by Bennett (C. & H. 1961). *Range:* Widespread in central and southern Chile and Argentina between sea level and about 6,000 ft., from 27 to 55°S and on Staten I. It migrates north in autumn (March) and then occurs from the coast of Brazil to Peru between 2° and 10°S.

Rufous-tailed Plantcutter

Phytotoma rara Molina

One adult female in rather worn plumage was found skulking among bushes being shadowed by a Falkland Thrush, at Douglas Station on 12th March 1937 (Hamilton 1939). *Range:* Well known in central Chile (28–43°S) from the coast to about 6,000 ft. in valleys of the Andean foothills; also occurs in Argentina from 36–42°S. Some northerly migration of the southern populations is thought to take place.

Yellow-bridled Finch

Melanodera xanthogramma (G. R. Gray)

The earliest records of this species in the Falkland Is. were those of Darwin in 1833–34. He observed that it '. . . is common at the Falkland Is. and it often occurs mingled in the same flock with the last one.' (Black-throated Finch, *Melanodera melanodera*, which he stated was '. . . extremely abundant in large scattered flocks . . .'). Darwin went on to observe that these two species 'have a very close general resemblance', and gave excellent descriptions of the differences in plumage between males of the two species. He obviously could distinguish one from the other. Darwin suspected that the Yellow-bridled '. . . more commonly frequents higher parts of the hills.' This suggested habitat preference may indicate that there was a difference in diet between them. It is possible that the Yellow-bridled Finch depended on seeds of Fachine, a shrub formerly abundant, but which has now almost disappeared.

Less than thirty years later (about 1860), Abbott (quoted by Crawshay 1907) stated that the Black-throated Finch was plentiful everywhere, but that he knew nothing of the second 'so-called species of the genus', and 'I do not believe it different from the former', i.e. the Black-throated. Perhaps the Yellow-bridled had disappeared by 1860 or Captain Abbott failed to recognize it and was unfortunate in not obtaining a specimen. There have been none certainly recorded since Darwin's visits, although Hamilton thought he saw one in a flock of Black-throated Finches (C. & H. 1961). The Yellow-bridled Finch *may* still occur in small numbers, but it is unlikely to be recognized unless all male *Melanodera*-finches are examined closely. *Range:* Two races inhabit southern South America. *M. x. barrosi* (which has white tail edges) occurs in the Andes to about 10,000 ft. from 33°S in Chile and 36°S in Argentina to the Magellan Straits (53°S). *M. x. xanthogramma* (which has yellow tail edges) occurs only in Tierra del Fuego, Staten I. and the southern Magellanic islands to Cape Horn.

Appendix: Scientific Names of Plants and Animals

according to various authors, mainly Pettingill (1962).

Local Name	Scientific Name
Barberry	Berberis sp.
Box	Veronica elliptica
Brown Top	Agrostis tenuis
Chickweed	Stellaria media
Cinnamon Grass	Hierochloe magellanica
Currant	Ribes sp.
Cypress	Cupressus macrocarpa
Diddle-dee	Empetrum rubrum
Fachine	Chiliotrichum diffusum
Fern	Blechnum sp.
Giant Kelp	Macrocystis pyrifera and Lessonia sp.
Gorse	Ulex europaeus
Lichen	Lichenes sp.
Meadow-grass sp.	Poa annua?
Mosses	Sphagnum sp.
Mountain berry	Pernettya pumila
Mountain Blue Grass	Poa antarctica
Pigvine	Gunnera magellanica
Reed (? Brown Swamp Rush)	(Rostkovia magellanica)
Sand Cabbage	Leuceria suaveolens
Sand grass	Ammophila sp.?
Small Rush	Juncus scheuchzerioides
Sorrel	Rumex sp.
Tea berry	Myrteola nummularia
Thrift	Armeria sp.
Tussock-grass	Poa flabellata
White grass	Cortaderia pilosa
Wild Celery	Apium australa
Wild Strawberry	Rubus geoides
Willow	Salix sp.
Yorkshire Fog	Holcus lanatus

Local Name	Scientific Name
Blowfly	Calliphora sp.
Camel-cricket	Parudenus sp.
Cuttlefish	Cephalopoda sp.
Elephant Seal	Mirounga leonina
Guanaco	Lama guanicoe
Hare	Lepus europaeus
House Mouse	Mus musculus
Limpet	Patella sp.
Lobster-krill	Munida sp.
Moths	Noctuidae sp.
Mullet	Mugil sp.
Mussel	Mytilus sp.
Rabbit	Oryctolagus cuniculus
Rat (Brown)	Rattus norvegicus
Rock-cod	Notothenia sp.
Sandhoppers	Amphipoda sp.
Silver Fox	Canidae sp.
Smelt	Atherinichthys sp.
Southern Sea Lion	Otaria byronia
Squid	Cephalopoda sp.
Warrah/Falkland Fox	Dusicyon antarcticus-australis

Bibliography

Abbott, C. C., 1860. *The Penguins of the Falkland Islands*. Ibis, Vol. 2, No. 8: 336–8.

Alexander, W. B., 1955. *Birds of the Ocean*. Putnam, London.

Beck, R. H., 1918. *Photographs of Falkland Island bird life*. Bird Lore, Vol. 20, No. 1: 1–8.

Bennett, A. G., 1925. *The question of birds becoming rare and their protection*. Emu, Vol. 25, Part 1: 29–31.

———. 1926. *A List of the Birds of the Falkland Islands and Dependencies*. Ibis, 12th Series, No. 2: 306–33.

———. 1930. *Nesting of the Grey-backed Storm-Petrel. (Garrodia nereis chubbi)*. Oologists Record, Vol. 10, No. 4: 79.

———. 1931. *First record of a Humming-bird in the Falkland Islands*. Ibis, 13th Series, Vol. 1, No. 2: 348–9.

———. 1931. *Additional notes. . . .* to 1926 List. Ibis, 13th Series, Vol. 1: 12–13.

———. 1935. *Two records from the Falkland Islands*. Ibis, 13th Series, Vol. 5, No. 2: 436.

———. 1937. Coccyzus melanocoryphus *in the Falkland Islands*. Ibis, 14th Series, Vol. 1, No. 4: 868.

———. 1938. *Bartram's Sandpiper on the Falkland Islands*. Ibis, 14th Series, Vol. 2, No. 4: 764.

Bertrand, K., 1968. *Carcass Island 1765–1967*, in Thompson, W. H. (Ed.) The Falkland Islands Journal No. 2.

Brooks, W. S., 1917. *Notes on some Falkland Islands birds*. Bulletin of Mus. Comp. Zool. Harvard, Vol. 61, No. 7: 135–60.

Cawkell, E. M., 1960. Chapter on *Bird Life* in Cawkell, Maling and Cawkell 1960.

——— and Hamilton, J. E., 1961. *The Birds of the Falkland Islands*. Ibis, Vol. 103a, No. 1: 1–27.

———. Unpublished notes from the original draft of the above 1961 paper.

Cawkell, M. B. R., Maling, D. H. and Cawkell, E. M., 1960. *The Falkland Islands*. Macmillan, London.

Chapman, F. M., 1934. *Descriptions of new birds from Mocha Island, Chile, and the Falkland Islands. . . .* Amer. Mus. Nov. No. 762, (pp. 6–8 on some Falkland Islands species).

Cobb, A. F., 1910. *Wild Life in the Falklands*. Gowan's Nature Books, London.

———. 1933. *Birds of the Falkland Islands*. Witherby, London.

Colony of the Falkland Islands, 1964, No. 8. The Nature Reserves Ordinance.

Colony of the Falkland Islands, 1964, No. 15. The Wild Animals and Birds Protection Ordinance.

Crawshay, R., 1907. *The Birds of Tierra del Fuego*. Bernard Quaritch, London.

Dabbene, R., 1923. *Los Petreles y los Albatros del Atlantico Austral*. El Hornero Vol. III, No. 1: 1–33, 125–58.

Delacour, J. and Scott, P., 1954–64. *The Waterfowl of the World*. Four vols. Country Life, London.

Falla, R. A., 1934. *The distribution and breeding habits of petrels in northern New Zealand*. Rec. Auck. Inst. Mus. 1, No. 5: 245–60, as quoted in Murphy, 1936.

———, Sibson, R. B. and Turbott. E. G., 1966. *A Field Guide to the Birds of New Zealand*. Collins, London.

Fisher, J., 1954. *Bird Recognition* Vol. 1. Penguin books, London.

Gilliard, E. T., 1958. *Living Birds of the World*. Hamish Hamilton, London.

Goodall, J. D., Johnson, A. W. and Philippi, Dr. R. A. b, 1951 and 1957. *Las Aves de Chile*, Two vols. and supplement. Platt Establecimientos Graficos, Buenos Aires.

Gould, J. and Darwin, C., 1838–41. *The Zoology of the Voyage of H.M.S. 'Beagle', Part 3, Birds*. London.

Gould, J., 1859. *List of birds from the Falkland Islands, with descriptions of the eggs of some species, from specimens collected principally by Captain C. C. Abbott*. Proc. Zool. Soc. London, Part 27: 93–8.

Hamilton, J. E., 1934. *The sub-antarctic forms of the Great Skua* (Catharacta skua skua). Discovery Reports, Vol. 9: 161–74.

———. 1937. *The Chilean Skua in the Falkland Islands*. Ibis, 14th Series, Vol. 1, No. 1: 177–8.

———. 1939. *Additions to the Falkland Islands list*. Ibis, 14th Series, Vol. 3, No. 1: 139–40.

———. 1944. *The House-Sparrow in the Falkland Islands*. Ibis, Vol. 86: 553–4.

———. 1945. *First record of* Pterodroma mollis (*Gould*) *in the Falkland Islands*. Ibis, Vol. 87: 569–70.

———. 1950. *Addition to the Falkland Islands list*. Ibis, Vol. 92, No. 1: 146.

———. 1951. *The breeding place of* Pachyptila belcheri *Mathews*. Ibis, Vol. 93, No. 1: 139–40.

———. 1954. *The Emperor Penguin in the Falklands*. Ibis, Vol. 96, No. 2: 315.

Harrison, P. P. O., 1962. *Sea Birds of the South Pacific*. Royal Naval Birdwatching Society and H. G. Walters, Narberth.

Hattersley-Smith, G. and Hamilton, J. E., 1950. *A Recent Deposit of Bird Bones on the Falkland Is*. Nature, Vol. 166, No. 4213.

Hudson, W. H., 1920. *Birds of La Plata*. Two vols. London.

Ingham, S. E., 1959. *Banding of Giant Petrels by the Australian National Antarctic Research Expeditions 1955–1958*. Emu, Vol. 59: 189–200.

Jones, N. V., 1963. *The Sheathbill* Chionis alba (*Gmelin*) *at Signy Island, South Orkney Islands*. British Antarctic Survey Bulletin No. 2.

Kinnear, N. B., 1931. *Swallow-tailed Flycatcher in the Falkland Islands*. Ibis, 13th Series, Vol. 1, No. 3: 578.

Landsborough Thomson, A. (Ed.), 1964. *A New Dictionary of Birds*. Nelson, London.

Lowe, P. R., 1934. *On the evidence for the existence of two species of Steamer Duck (Tachyeres), and primary and secondary flightlessness in birds*. Ibis, 13th Series, Vol. 4, No. 3: 467–95.

Maling, D. H., 1960. Chapters on *Geology, Climate* and *Vegetation* in Cawkell, Maling and Cawkell 1960.

Mathews, G. M., 1931. *The nidification of two sea-birds*. Ibis, 13th Series, Vol. 1, No. 3: 571–2.

———. 1939. *Two new races of petrel*. Bull. B.O.C., Vol. 59: 103–4.

Meyer de Schaunsee, R., 1971. *A Guide to the Birds of South America*. Oliver & Boyd, Edinburgh.

Moody, R. C., 1842. *Despatch from Lieutenant Governor Moody to Lord Stanley*; reprinted in Thompson, W. H. (Ed.) 1969. The Falkland Islands Journal No. 3.

Murphy, R. C., 1936. *Oceanic Birds of South America*. Two vols. Macmillan and American Museum of Natural History, New York.

Olrog, C. C., 1959. *Las Aves Argentinas*, Una Guia de Campo. Universidad Nacional de Tucuman, Instituto 'Miguel Lillo'.

Peterson, R., Mountfort, G. and Hollom, P. A. D., 1954. *A Field Guide to the Birds of Britain and Europe*. Collins, London.

Pettingill, E. R., 1962. *Penguin Summer*. Cassell, London.

Pettingill, O. S. jr., 1960. *The Effects of Climate and Weather on the Birds of the Falkland Islands*. Proc. XIIth International Ornithological Congress, Helsinki 1958, pp. 604–14.

———. 1973. *Passerine Birds of the Falkland Is.*, in The Living Bird, Vol. 12. Cornell Laboratory of Ornithology, New York.

Phillips, J. A., 1916. *A new form of* Chloephaga hybrida. Auk, n.s. Vol. 33, No. 4: 423–4.

Reid, R. Unpublished notes on birds of George, Bleaker, Speedwell and other islands, 1961.

Reynolds, P. W., 1932. *Notes on the Birds of Snipe, and the Woodcock Islands, in the Beagle Channel*. Ibis, 13th Series, Vol. 2, No. 1: 34–39.

———. 1935. *Notes on the Birds of Cape Horn*. Ibis, 13th Series, Vol. 5, No. 1: 65–101.

Rowan, M. K., 1952. *The Greater Shearwater* (Puffinus gravis) *at its Breeding Grounds*. Ibis, Vol. 94, No. 1: 97–121.

Sclater, P. L., 1860. *Catalogue of the birds of the Falkland Islands*. Proc. Zool. Soc. London, part 28: 382–91.

——— and Sharpe, R. B. *et al.*, 1885–98. *Catalogue of Birds in the British Museum*, Vols. X–XV and XXIII–XXVII. London.

———. 1895. *Exhibition by Philip Lutley Sclater of skin of* Phalaropus wilsoni *from the Falkland Islands*. Ibis, 7th Series, Vol. 1, No. 1: 145.

Scott, P., 1957. *A Coloured Key to the Wildfowl of the World*. The Wildfowl Trust, Slimbridge.

Sladen, W. J. L., 1952. *Notes on methods of marking Penguins*. Ibis, 94: 541–3.

——— and Penney, R. L., 1960. *Penguin flipper-bands used by the United States Antarctic Research Program, Bird-banding Program 1958–60*. Bird-banding, Vol. XXXI: 79–82.

———. (1961). *Antarctic Ornithology*, Ch. VII of Science in Antarctica, Pt. 1, The

Life Sciences in Antarctica. Publication 839, National Academy of Sciences—National Research Council.

Sladen, W. J. L. and Tickell, W. L. N., 1958. *Antarctic Bird-banding by the Falkland Islands Dependencies Survey 1945–1957*. Bird-banding, Vol. XXIX, No. 1: 1–26.

Strange, I. J., 1965. *Beauchene Island*. The Polar Record, Vol. 12, No. 81: 725–30

———. 1968. *A Breeding Colony of* Pachyptila turtur *in the Falkland Islands*. Ibis, Vol. 110, No. 3: 358–9.

Swales, M. K., 1965. *The sea-birds of Gough Island*. Ibis, Vol. 107, No. 1: 17–42, No. 2: 215–29.

Swann, H. K., 1924–30. *A Monograph of the Birds of Prey*. Two vols. British Museum (Natural History), London.

Tickell, W. L. N., 1962. *The Dove Prion* Pachyptila desolata *Gmelin*. Falkland Islands Dependencies Survey Scientific Reports, No. 33.

———. 1965. *New records for South Georgia*. Ibis, Vol. 107, No. 3: 388–9.

——— and Cordall, P. A., 1960. *South Georgia Biological Expedition 1958–9, Elsehul and Bird Island*. Unpublished report to F.I.D.S.

——— and Scotland, C. D., 1961. *Recoveries of ringed Giant Petrels* Macronectes giganteus, Ibis, Vol. 103a, No. 2: 260–6.

——— and Woods, R. W., 1972. *Ornithological Observations at sea in the South Atlantic Ocean, 1954–64*. British Antarctic Survey Bulletin, No. 31, Dec. 1972.

———. (No date). *Report of the Bird-banding Expedition to Bird Island, South Georgia 1960–61*, U.S.A.R.P.

Vallentin, R., 1924. *Birds* in *The Falkland Islands* by V. F. Boyson, Clarendon Press, Oxford.

Westerskov, K., 1960. *Birds of Campbell Island*. Wildlife Publication No. 61, New Zealand Dept. of Internal Affairs.

Witherby, H. F. *et al* 1940–41. *The Handbook of British Birds*, Five vols. H. F. and G Witherby, London.

Woods, R. W., 1970(a). *The Avian Ecology of a Tussock island in the Falkland Islands*. Ibis, Vol. 112, No. 1: 15–24.

———. 1970(b). *Great Shearwater* Puffinus gravis *breeding in the Falkland Islands*. Ibis, Vol. 112, No. 2: 259–60.

Young, C. D., 1967. *The Natural Vegetation of the Falklands*, in Thompson, W. H. (Ed.) 1967. The Falkland Islands Journal No. 1.

Zotta, A. R., 1944. *Lista Sistematica de las Aves Argentinas*. Museo Argentino de Ciencias Naturales, Buenos Aires.

Index

The figures in bold type refer to the Field Guide, figures in italic type refer to illustrations.